Mind the Gender Gap

FEMINIST DEVELOPMENTS IN VIOLENCE AND ABUSE

Series Editors: Dr Hannah Bows, Durham University, UK and Professor Nicole Westmarland, Durham University, UK

Feminist Developments in Violence and Abuse provides a feminist forum for academic work that pushes forward existing knowledge around violence and abuse, informing policy and practice, with the overarching objective of contributing towards ending violence and abuse within our society. The series enables academics, practitioners, policymakers and professionals to continually build and explore their understanding of the dynamics, from the micro- to the macro-level, that are driving violence and abuse. The study of abuse and violence has a large scope for co-producing research, and this series is a home for research involving a broad range of stakeholders; particularly those working in grassroots domestic and sexual violence organisations, police, prosecutors, lawyers, campaign groups, housing and victim services. As violence and abuse research reaches across disciplinary boundaries, the series has an interdisciplinary scope with research impact at the heart.

Available Volumes:

Forthcoming Volumes:

Feminist Developments in Violence and Abuse

Mind the Gender Gap: A Mobilities Perspective of Sexual Harassment on the London Underground

BY

SIÂN LEWIS
University of Plymouth, UK

emerald
PUBLISHING

United Kingdom – North America – Japan – India – Malaysia – China

Emerald Publishing Limited
Emerald Publishing, Floor 5, Northspring, 21-23 Wellington Street, Leeds LS1 4DL.

First edition 2024

An electronic version of this book is freely available, thanks to the
support of libraries working with Knowledge Unlatched. KU is a
collaborative initiative designed to make high quality books Open
Access for the public good. More information about the initiative
and links to the Open Access version can be found at www.
knowledgeunlatched.org

Reprints and permissions service
Contact: www.copyright.com

British Library Cataloguing in Publication Data
A catalogue record for this book is available from the British Library

ISBN: 978-1-83753-029-8 (Print)
ISBN: 978-1-83753-026-7 (Online)
ISBN: 978-1-83753-028-1 (Epub)

INVESTOR IN PEOPLE

For Dad

Contents

Acknowledgements

I want to start by acknowledging the women whose experiences are the foundation of this book. Thank you for sharing your stories with me so candidly. I hope I've done justice to them.

The writing of this book coincided with a rough time. As such, these acknowledgements are for those who have cheerleaded me through the writing process *and* acted as big soft pillows of support in a period of heavy grief. I feel deeply lucky to have so many loving friends who show up in abundance to hang out in the trenches, and to celebrate the wins – including the writing of this book. Life would be crap without you all.

A special mention to Fiona, you are an exceptional friend to me, Mum to Nia, and an all-round wonderful human being. Ricky. Thanks doesn't begin to cover it. I don't have the words to show my gratitude for how you've kept me afloat, and let me sink without judgement when I needed to. You are the most genuine person I know and I count myself incredibly lucky that we're muddling through and growing together. You know i'd rather be damned with you. Both of you have held so much of my storm (especially over the last year) and I am so very grateful. Mum and Annie, I'm sure that you are the best people in the world, and I'm endlessly inspired by your softness and resilience. Nick, I'm so glad you're part of our family.

A heartfelt thank you to Oliver – for always picking up the phone, and for being so generous with your intellect, advice and reassurance. It has made all the difference, and I would have struggled without it. Iain, thanks for your collegiate kindness, workday coffees and cold swims to clear our busy heads. Every team needs someone like you. Janina, for the daily T. Callie, for your proofreading and words of encouragement, and to Paula Saukko, for your supervision of this research project, and pushing me to think laterally.

And Dad, for a lifetime of unconditional love and support. I have so desperately missed you not being here whilst writing this. You would have been disproportionately, embarrasingly proud. To make up for it, I'll be extra proud of myself.

Chapter 1

Introduction: Arrhythmia and Egg Yolk

Abstract

Using a mobilities framework, this book aims to tell the stories of sexual harassment on the London Underground not as a single, exceptional moment, but as part of women's wider urban experiences and movements through public urban life. The way this book is structured attempts to mirror and portray this. As such, the chapters that follow this one take such an approach: the before, the during and the after. Prior to this, two chapters are dedicated to the theoretical and conceptual underpinnings that are employed to make sense of women's experiences. In this introductory chapter, I overview the issue of sexual harassment on public transport more broadly. I situate the phenomenon in its social context of a global endemic of violence against women, before zooming in to 'set the scene' of the London Underground. I will briefly outline the conceptual framework I use to understand sexual harassment on the London Underground and summarise how situating the issue at the axis of mobilities, rhythms, space and time, allows new insights into how sexual harassment happens 'on the move'. I then summarise the methodological approach taken for the research that constitutes this book, including a consideration of researcher positionality and ethics. I also make a case for the value of 'messy' qualitative, reflexive approaches, and how this is essential for disrupting normative and 'taken for granted' conceptions of sexual harassment. I argue that, by giving space to the complexity of women's in-depth, kinetic stories, we are rewarded with a deeper understanding of the anticipation, manifestation and reaction to incidents of sexual harassment on public transport.

Keywords: Sexual harassment; public transport; London Underground; mobilities; qualitative methods

Early Autumn 2013, Istanbul, Turkey

The air on the Metrobus is dense and heavy. It's only 8am but the sun is unseasonably warm as it glares into the carriage in slow interludes through the dusty windows. As we're shuttled from the belly of the city towards its fringes, the intense smog seeps in through cracks and fuses with the odours of hasty bodies that occupy the early morning rush hours. The collective agitation on the carriage is palpable, as individual cadences are subsumed into the broader rhythms of the city. In a metropolis of over 15 million people, breathing space is a rare luxury, and, like every other working day, we're crammed in like rigid Tetris blocks – thigh to hip, elbow to back, shoulder to armpit. We don't know each other, we probably won't see each other again, and the only thing we have in common is the direction of our commute. Yet in this moment I'm physically closer to the strangers on this bus than I have been to most people I know. I still find it unsettling, but over the past few months, instead of occupying a state of constant vigilance towards my surroundings, I've gradually developed the knack of zoning out from the overwhelming urban stimulus bubbling around me. This has the added benefit of perceptually speeding up the hour-long journey and taking my mind off my aching feet. I breathe in deeply and close my eyes, one arm stretched above my head, fingers tense and clasping the handrail, while the rest of me groggily sways back and forth in keeping with the rhythm of the static bodies around me ....

Back and forth
    Back and forth
        Back and forth
            Back and forth

I'm dislodged from the metronomic motion, not suddenly, but gradually, like a morning alarm softly invading a dream before wrenching you from it. I become aware of a dull, hard, intermittent pressure against the small of my back, that feels...out of place somehow, even in the sardine crush of bodies. An inconsiderate elbow? Someone's bag? Even before I force myself to steal a cautious glance behind me, I *know* what's happening. My *body* knows what's happening. My heart flips into arrhythmia, my stomach churns, and my muscles freeze. But when I turn my head slowly, I see that the man pressed up behind me is looking off to the side distractedly, rather than directly at me. This confuses me enough to make me question whether this is *really* happening. Is he *really* pushing his erection into my back, or am I imagining it? I know with certainty what is happening, and yet I am unsure.

In this liminal state, I don't move. I don't react. I don't make a scene. I don't know how long I stand like this – time morphs, swells, and stretches until we pull into the next station and, amongst the flux of passengers alighting and arriving, I manage to shift my body away from him as the carriage reconfigures itself. He doesn't look at me once. The queasiness lingers in the pit of my stomach, but as the indifferent Metrobus shuttles us on, it's *almost* like nothing happened at all.

2018, London, UK

I'm riding on the top deck of the 176 bus to meet a friend on Lower Marsh, a market street nestled down to the side of Waterloo station. It's a late spring morning and the bus is relatively empty, hosting only a scattering of people and an unusually calm ambiance that is entirely removed from the chaotic and jumbled medley of London rush hours. The 40-minute journey is a route I know like the back of my hand and a distracted glance out of the window is all I need to get my bearings. The pleasure in this is that I can daydream, read my book and actually enjoy the journey. In moments like these, travel becomes not time wasted and hurried along, but a time-space in which doing *nothing* is perfectly acceptable because, by travelling, you are already doing *something*.

In this relaxed state, I distantly register someone in my periphery moving from further back on the bus and sitting behind me. Strange, on an almost empty bus, but I don't really think much of it. I check my phone absentmindedly for messages and get back to my book. Minutes later, I'm pulled back to the bus again when I sense shuffling behind me. The man who had moved from the back has changed seats again to sit directly across the aisle from me. My skin prickles and I feel myself shift from relaxed to wary and cautious. I can sense something's not *quite* right. He's looking at me. With my head down, I glance across to my left and as I do, he turns to look ahead, avoiding my gaze. But … I can see he's touching himself, slowly, over the top of his khaki trousers, making no real attempt to disguise it. My stomach somersaults theatrically, as I quickly look away. As I do, I feel his gaze burn back towards me. When I look again, he's staring straight forwards. Caught in a bizarre back and forth, I try to meet his eye, to give him a look that says, I see you, I'm furious and this is not ok. My heart thuds in my chest, my blood feels thick like egg yolk, whilst my brain whirs at a hundred miles an hour. I know that in a few minutes we'll arrive at my stop. I'll press the red square that will ping loudly, telling the driver in his booth that someone needs to get off the bus, and I'll balance my way down the stairs, grabbing the handrail as it jerks forward, as if this stop is unexpected. I'll alight through the middle doors. I'll get on with my day… Or, I can say something now, confront him, express my inner outrage directly, an outrage that is not just about him, but built from an accumulation of experiences of men causing my skin to crawl and making me feel like my safety is precarious and my freedom restricted. This is what I want to do, I think. But in the moment, vocalising seems impossible, outside the realm of my options. I don't feel scared, but stifled, restrained by the social norms of public transport (which is funny, I think, when a man is masturbating at me in broad daylight on the 176). I could point my phone at him, take a photo and say I'm going to report him to the police, scare him, so he doesn't do this to another woman or girl. In a split second, I play out every possible chain of events triggered by every possible action I can take. It's not reactive, it's calculated. But at the same time, it's automatic, enmeshed in my psyche and entangled in a web of experience, both personal and vicarious, that culminate in the ability (and necessity?) to instantaneously measure and weigh up how to react to unwanted sexual attention from men. Out of my window to the right, I notice The Old Vic theatre up ahead. It's my stop. I press the red button, close my book and lift myself from my seat. As I leave, I try to catch his eye again, to win this game he's forced me to play, but his avoidance is obstinate, and I pull my gaze away from him like stubborn blue tack, giving into the fact that I have chosen to 'do nothing'.

*

In a biographical catalogue of experiences of unwanted, intrusive behaviour from men, these incidents have occupied a disproportionate amount of headspace and scrutiny. I felt guilty and confused by my lack of overt resistance, defiance or confrontation; things I had displayed many times in response to incidents of street harassment. I struggled to make sense of my own reactions, knowing only that labelling them as simple, carnal 'fear' responses felt like a reductive untruth. Confusion and apathy felt more fitting, but this jarred with my internalised script of how I should feel or act. Through the gradual development of a feminist, academic lens, I began to recognise that these incidents and my reactions could, *in part,* be understood within the broader context of fear and anxieties around gender-based violence in public space. Women are often told that our level of fear of sexual violence has no logical basis in the modern western world; that we are afforded equal rights, freedoms and security. And yet we are simultaneously subject to repeated interpersonal experiences and bombarded with prolific media reporting of gendered violence around the globe and across social contexts. Additionally, violence against women is commodified and 'enjoyed' through the avid consumption of crime dramas and true crime (Havas & Horeck, 2021; Slakoff, 2022). This imperceptible merging of fact and fiction, visceral and vicarious, culminates in a ubiquitous sense of danger, running like an electric current under a thin veneer of freedom, safety and security. Subsequently, in our unwanted interactions with men, we often fear the worst and act accordingly. Our underlying objective when negotiating experiences of sexual harassment and assault is often driven by the perceived need to avoid an escalation into violence (Fileborn & O'Neill, 2023). As such, it's no surprise that the impact of fear dominates academic discussion around sexual harassment.

However, reflecting on my experiences on the Istanbul and London buses, I realised it wasn't fear that entirely, or even predominantly dictated my reactions. It was more understated. Subtle. I felt uneasy and awkward speaking out on the quiet bus. I didn't want to make a fuss or draw attention to myself. I also just wanted to get to where I was going. I didn't want to be disrupted. I didn't want these actions to leak into the day and beyond, inflate in prominence and consume my time and headspace. I wanted to keep it contained and get on with my journey and my day. As I began the research that constitutes this book and started speaking to women about their experiences of unwanted male attention on public transport, specifically the London Underground network, I heard versions of my own stories mirrored back to me time and time again. I found myself subconsciously nodding in understanding as the women I spoke to grappled to articulate the complexities and contradictions that seem to dominate these moments and their subsequent impact. This was particularly true when they deviated from the normative scripts of feisty, feminist responses, or inaction caused by a sense of female vulnerability and fear.

We spoke about incidents of harassment and assault on the London Underground that were various and multitudinous in form and perceived severity. In each of the stories I heard, it became clear that there was something particular about the way these incidents were perpetrated, experienced and reacted to that was unmistakeably linked with their taking place in a public transport environment and the social norms and regulations bound up in these spaces. Being 'on the move' was the thread of similarity that weaved lucidly through these stories, moulding how these behaviours were enacted, and warping women's reactions and responses to them.

> It bred the uncertainty, even as a hand moved between her legs, as to whether she was really being assaulted.

> It meant he could put both of his hands on her hips from behind, squeezing her tightly as he moved her to the side so he could pass, innocuous and unnoticed by other passengers.

> It allowed the man next her to lean forward and subtly place his smart phone to take a photo up her skirt.

> It facilitated the man who, on a packed city tube, cupped his hand between her legs, moving back and forth on the outside of her trousers.

It meant that, when she got to the bottom of the escalator and realised the man who had been standing a bit too close behind her had ejaculated on her coat, he had already disappeared into the crowd.

It allowed the strange man next to her on an evening tube to silently take her hand from her lap and put it on his, holding it tightly, as she froze in shock.

It meant that on a packed morning rush hour tube, the business-man standing behind her could put both of his hands firmly on her bum and when confronted, simply remove them and act like it was an accident.

It impacted on why, when she rejected a man who was flirting with her on the night tube and he stood over her calling her a fucking bitch, no one else in the carriage said a word.

It meant the man wearing a thick coat on a hot day, who squeezed behind her on a busy carriage, could rub his erection against her leg, causing enough confusion that she didn't speak out.

It permitted the man who masturbated at her in an empty carriage when she was on her way home from after school club, to do so for over five minutes, without her being able to leave.

These examples illustrate the variety of experiences of sexual harassment and assault on the London Underground that happened to some of the women I spoke to. Situated in a broader culture endemic of sexual and gender-based violence, these incidents on public transport deserve their own critique and understandings. The space, its physicality and design, its purpose, its rhythms and the social interactions and norms that occur within it, all coalesce to create an atmosphere and social space in which sexual harassment is perpetrated, experienced, negotiated and remembered in ways that are uniquely mitigated by the very nature of this mobile environment. It is these experiences and the specificity of the transport environment that are the focus of this book. In an attempt to portray the complexities of women's subjective experiences of sexual harassment and assault within the context of the London Underground, I take a 'whole journey' approach (discussed further below in notes on methodology). In Chapter 4, I focus on the '*before*' and explore how women experience and negotiate London and the Underground in everyday life. Chapter 5 addresses the '*during*', going into detail about the incident of harassment or assault to understand the key features of women's experiences in a transport environment. Chapter 6 looks at '*after*' the event to understand how women negotiate the memory of sexual harassment, and how it impacts their mobilities over time.

Sexual Harassment 'On the Move': A Mobilities Perspective

Whilst this book focusses on how public transport shapes experiences of sexual harassment, it does not presume or intend to insinuate that the way transport is structured is the primary, underlying cause of this form of sexual violence. Underpinning this work is the acknowledgement and understanding that this harmful behaviour is located within a global endemic of gender-based violence (WHO, 2021), with an estimated one in three women experiencing at least one incident of physical or sexual violence in their lifetime. Predominantly perpetrated by men against women, feminist work has extensively theorised sexual harassment as a pervasive part of everyday gendered life, or as Liz Kelly (1987) suggests, as part of the continuum of sexual violence. A 2021 investigation by the United Nations Women UK found that in the UK, 97% of women aged 18–24 have experienced sexual harassment. Acknowledged in this way, sexual harassment can be understood as a widely normalised behaviour that exists on a continuum that connects these intrusions with intimate partner violence and 'stranger' rape. In this way, rather than focussing on and isolating experiences of extreme sexual violence as episodic and deviant, they can be understood as part of the everyday, normative context of women's lives, located in patriarchal structures that permit their occurrence within society. The perpetration of sexual harassment across various social arenas has been widely explored: including private and public spaces such as the workplace (Spiliopoulou & Whitcomb, 2023), the streets (Fileborn & O'Neill, 2023), the night-time economy (Gunby et al., 2020) and music festivals (Bows et al., 2024). Research has identified that the extent and type of sexual harassment are significantly shaped by the context in which it occurs (Madan & Nalla, 2016) and that the way in which women react to harassment is, in part, influenced by the distinct nature of the environment in which it is experienced (Krasas & Henson, 1997).

Unsurprisingly, the perpetration and experience of sexual harassment on transport differ from other arenas, and yet, until relatively recently, had received little academic attention, particularly in the global West. Consequently, the uniqueness of experiences within these spaces has often been obfuscated by conflating them with public spaces such as the streets. As with other spaces, patriarchal sociocultural norms and gender stereotypes underpin women's use of transport systems and interactions that occur within them. Therefore, whilst sexual harassment occurs on transport around the globe, the scope and frequency of the issue varies, and is particularly prevalent in countries where gender equality remains disparate, and whose transport environments therefore remain hostile and less gender-responsive to the needs and experiences of women and girls (Noor & Iamtrakul, 2023). Exploring the specific nature of sexual harassment in different contexts exposes how the normative social interactions within that space impact how incidents of sexual violence are perpetrated and experienced. However, whilst *space* is important here, I contend that there are other aspects that have a significant influence, including *mobility, temporality* and *rhythm*. Significantly, by viewing this phenomenon through the lens of movement or *mobility,* new insights and deeper understandings of the experiences of sexual harassment on public transport can be established. Previously overlooked as a 'neutral set of technologies and processes' (Larsen et al., 2006, p. 3), encounters that occurred within a travel environment were omitted from analysis. As such, the 'mobilities turn' (Urry, 2000) connected social sciences with transport approaches, and through a focus on the collisions of time and space, drew attention to the complexity of the movement of people and things in the social world. Mobilities studies have focussed on the social interactions that are implicated by various forms of travel, including public transport in urban spaces (Bissell, 2018; Urry, 2007). A mobilities perspective urges us to acknowledge and confront the complexities of transport environments and the role they play in social interactions (including sexual harassment), rather than view them as an inert and neutral backdrop.

Forming part of the ontological fabric and functioning of a city, public transportation systems enable the movement of people and connect the various social spheres of urban life. And yet they are also liminal spaces, existing beyond the domains of work, leisure and home and the static streets. This liminality is at least in part due to their abundant mobility and 'unfixed' nature. Understanding the way in which these systems are perceived and experienced is fundamental to a deeper, clearer comprehension of instances of sexual violence that occur within them. As well as taking a mobilities approach to understand gendered experience, this also means it is essential to *take a gendered approach to understanding mobilities*, or in other words, to consider how mobility and the use of transport are gendered.

These dynamics will be further explored in Chapter 3, which outlines a mobilities perspective and its value. It also overviews the conceptual framework used to make sense of sexual harassment in a public transport environment. This framework consists of space, mobilities, rhythms and temporalities and throughout this book these concepts will be applied to understand women's experiences of sexual harassment in transport: how they pre-empt these acts of gendered violence, experience and react to them 'in the moment', how they are remembered and negotiated over time, and how this impacts their urban mobilities. A mobilities perspective helps theorise and analyse the obvious (yet neglected) fact that these experiences are occurring in a transitory space and that this significantly influences how they are anticipated, perpetrated, experienced and responded to. This subsequently impacts women's use of transport and broader urban mobilities. In short, this book aims to offer a much-needed explanation of the particularities and impact of sexual harassment happening *on the move*.

Setting the Scene: London and the London Underground

This book focusses on experiences of sexual harassment on the London Underground. The decision to focus on this city and network arose from a number of reasons. Academically, very few studies of sexual harassment on transport have focussed on Western cities. As highlighted below in more detail, Transport for London (TfL), the Underground's governing body, and the British Transport Police had recently begun to show significant interest in the gendered experiences on their services, particularly the prevalence of unwanted sexual attention in the capital city. I recognised that there was both a need and appetite for qualitative research in this subject area. My geographical proximity to the city also influenced the decision. At the time I was living in the East Midlands and London was easily accessible by train. However, shortly after beginning the research I relocated to London in 2016. I wanted to immerse myself and be part of the city, to use the transport network I was writing about. The way a city is built and structured intimately guides the movements and interactions of those living within it and I wanted to be part of this, to feel and experience the flow, rhythms and sociabilities of the city. My early fieldnotes capture these sensations:

> For the first few weeks in the capital city everything is wonderfully new and alarmingly frenzied. The tempo feels inconsistent, I repeatedly underestimate the vastness of the city and am constantly running late. The vivid visual chaos of the city distracts and enchants me, consuming my senses and filling up the camera roll on my phone with images of red buses and postcard historical landmarks. I feel overwhelmed by the sheer number of people, whose proximity and ambivalence makes me feel both exposed and anonymous.

Urban sociologists have recognised that there is a distinct way of being and moving through the city that is associated with dense urban populations (Urry, 2007). Hubbard (2012, p. 6) considers how individualism and indifference often dominate, and attitudes that are seen as characteristic of modern cities include anonymity, voyeurism, consumption and motion. As such, interactions with strangers are often fleeting and superficial, though this should not be understood as mere arrogance or rudeness, rather as an urbanite coping strategy to manage the intensity of the city environment. This description is incredibly fitting for London, and particularly the Underground where the social atmosphere of 'civil inattention' (Goffman, 1963) is both visible and palpable. Widely considered one of the greatest metropolises in the world with its historical and modern landmarks, London can be considered what Lynch (1960) describes as a 'highly imageable city'; well-formed, distinct and remarkable, it occupies a space in the global imagination. With a population of approximately 8.9 million in 2022, and hosting 5,596 people per km^2, it is 15 times denser than the rest of England (Trust for London, 2024). On top of this, in 2021 the city hosted 7.8 million tourists (significantly less than before the COVID-19 pandemic, where in 2019 the city saw 21 million visitors; cityoflondon.gov.uk). Experiences of the city are as diverse as the people who occupy and visit it, as are experiences of the city's vast transport system, including its underground rail network.

Dating back to 1863, the London Underground, colloquially known as 'the Tube', is a vast public transport system that constitutes 11 different 'lines' covering 402 km and 272 stations and serving up to five million passenger journeys a day (Transport for London, 2024). The Tube occupies its own space in the global imagination, from congested rush hour carriages, to the famous 'mind the gap' announcements, to the roundel logo and Harry Beck's iconic topological Tube map.

As an essential part of the urban fabric of any city, transportation systems enable the movement of people and link activity across the city, connecting work, leisure and home. They have the potential to provide a glimpse into the culture of the city including interactions and risks, or as Ceccato and Uittenbogaard (2014) describe, transport has the capacity to reflect the dynamics of a city as a whole. The dyadic relationship between the city and the Underground is key to this work, and embodied and perceptual experiences of the city are the focus of Chapter 4. It further explores the everyday gendered mobilities in London *above* ground, understanding London not simply as a backdrop, but as a complex and active organism that impacts on experiences of sexual harassment in the transport network that runs beneath its surface. The research participant's experiences and descriptions of London are textured and varied, filled with warmth, fondness, hatred, exhaustion and ambivalence. They set the scene and start the journey towards a rich and contextualised exploration of experiences on the Underground.

To an outsider or a visitor, the London Underground can be experienced as confusing and intimidating, possessing the physical and atmospheric sense of the urban rat race, particularly during peak travel or 'rush hours'. It appears unrelenting and hostile, dominated by the rush and rhythm of unforgiving commuters (Bissell, 2010). So strong is this feeling that it does not take long before individual corporeal tempos are subsumed into the flow and pace of the Underground. My early fieldnotes describe this as an 'inexplicable force' or undercurrent that pulls you along with the wave of people. Yet despite this apparent stress and chaos, for those who know the rhythms of the city, it is a methodical, orderly and predictable part of the daily routine. After a few months in the city, I reflected on this in my fieldnotes:

> [...] as the city slowly reveals itself and I become orientated in my new environment, patterns and rhythms become distinctive and legible, the chaos becomes more ordered and consistent. I adapt, and my own paces and movements become subsumed into the city's haste. Headphones in, I hurry and jostle to and from places I am in no rush to get to, anxious urgency bubbling under my skin, pushing me through crowds and up escalators.

Women also spoke of 'invisible rules' and 'Tube etiquette', such as minimal eye contact, not talking to strangers, standing on the right side of the escalator and taking up as little space as possible in the carriages. One only has to take a single journey on the Tube to know these 'rules' apply and are largely self-governed by regular users. This can be seen as emblematic of modern urban society: strangers forced together in close proximity, acknowledgement of the other, without imposition, or to use Goffman's (1963) terminology again, this is an example of 'civil inattention'. These 'unwritten' social rules and the awareness of personal boundaries, largely facilitate the successful functioning of socio-spatial logistics. Yet there is a dark side to this functional apathy that risks breeding a lack of social responsibility towards others (Le Bon, 2004), or as we see later, a form of 'moral minimalism' (Baumgartner, 1988). Indeed, this metaphorical space and distance that civil inattention creates is highly functional in the perpetation of sexual harassment on the London Underground.

As discussed below, taking an ethnographic approach meant that I spent a significant amount of time travelling on the Underground, observing the space and taking detailed fieldnotes about often seemingly innocuous feelings and interactions, as well as exchanges with men that felt uncomfortable and intimidating. I remain steadfast in the view that, without engaging physically, sensorially, emotionally and intellectually with London and the Underground, much of the nuance and intricacies that existed in these spaces and in women's stories would never have revealed themselves. Only through immersion into the seemingly mundane, normal and everyday motions of the space could I understand women's experiences within it.

Notes on 'Messy' Methodologies

> *[...] disconnected and seemingly insignificant observations slowly add up and come together to form insightful thoughts and revealing themes. It's almost like a maths puzzle: you can't get the answer without doing the working out.* (Excerpt from reflexive journal)

What constitutes this research is an amalgamation of a wealth of data gathered through interviews, informal story-sharing and conversations, and my own experiences and ethnographic observations of the London Underground. The way the data were gathered and presented is significantly influenced by feminist epistemologies, including the centring of women's voices and visible incorporation of researcher reflexivity. The collection and collation of these data was, overall, an embodied, experiential and emotional engagement with the research topic and the process of knowledge production (Carroll, 2012). This approach may be considered 'messy' by those of a positivist disposition; however occupying an interpretivist stance allows space in research for how participants (and the researcher) subjectively interpret and make sense of the social world (Mason, 2002). At the axis of this book are the stories of women discussing, in detail, their lived experiences of sexual harassment or assault on the London Underground, drawing predominantly on in-depth, semi-structured interviews. These interviews mostly took place in cafes dotted around London (often in or next to train stations) over a few cups of overpriced coffee and lasted an hour or two. The style was fluid and conversational with a loose structure that encompassed the before, during and after of their experiences. This approach allowed incidents to be contextualised, avoiding reducing them to a single isolated moment or feeling and rather situating them as part of a personal biography, in broader gendered power relations and interactions with urban space. During many of the interviews, there were moments where interactions shifted into what felt like friendly and intimate conversation, taking diversions to briefly visit childhood dreams, family dynamics, ex-partners, health issues, and often, past incidents of sexual intrusions. What became apparent through this approach is the messiness, confusion and complexity that regularly accompany experiences of sexual harassment and assault. Indeed, many of the participants were seemingly reconfiguring and 'making sense' of their experiences as we spoke, memories reflecting and refracting through the lens of time passed and focussed conversation.

This 'whole journey' approach proffers not only to disrupt existing 'academic' knowledge of the dynamics of sexual harassment but also to challenge dominant approaches to understanding sexual harassment on transport in terms of methodologies. When I first began exploring existing work that focused on sexual violence on public transport, I noticed the absence of qualitative, particularly ethnographic, or observational approaches, a reflection that is mirrored by Ceccato et al. (2022). Instead, there has been a focus on understanding the prevalence of the issue and the proportion of women who have been victimised (Gekoski et al., 2015); understanding how many women report assaults to authorities; and the trajectory of these reports (Solymosi et al., 2017). This information seemed to be garnered largely through analysis of police data or quantitative surveys, analysed and presented in numerical form to offer a rapid assessment or a broad overview (Gekoski et al., 2015; Stringer, 2007). Whilst incredibly useful, particularly for practitioners, stakeholders and law enforcement to understand the scope of the issue, a statistical analysis cannot communicate the experiential subjectivity of an incident of sexual harassment or assault, or reflect the role of the social environment in which it occurred. Similarly, the meanings women place on these experiences and the subsequent impact they have on their mobilities and engagement with urban space are neglected or obscured in place of a simplified, macro, numerical perspective. Even when women's stories are situated at the centre of research as the subject, quantitative methods (such as large-scale surveys) run the risk of sanitising complex experiences for the sake of a large sample size and more generalisable conclusions and recommendations that provide palatable and 'valid' outputs in the realm of administrative and policy-driven agendas. Useful as this can be to get a 'bigger picture', it can strip experiences of victimisation of their messiness and remove them from context. Engaging with semi-structured interviews provides insight into subjective interpretations, perceptions, beliefs and meanings that the women attach to their experiences, going beyond what is easily visible and observable.

In this book, the formal interviews constitute a relatively small sample size of 29 women. This, in conjunction with the fact that this book focusses on one mode of transport, in one city, may leave it open to critiques of a lack of generalisability. However, I contend that the insights this book offers, both in its theoretical and methodological approach, as well as its findings, can be transferred and related to understanding sexual harassment in contexts beyond this one, particularly in other transport systems around the globe. An important consideration is highlighting the demographics of women whose voices make up the majority of this book. Stanley (2013, p. 21) discusses how, whilst feminist work has focussed on showing women's 'experiences of oppression', it is important to recognise that 'women' do not share an ontological existence or material reality, and their experiences are not unified. This has been particularly highlighted by black feminists who emphasise the need for feminist research to recognise difference in their analyses of women's experiences (Hill Collins, 1986; Lorde, 1984). Welsh et al. (2006) considered this in their research on diverse groups of women in Canada, highlighting that women's race and citizenship impacted how they defined their experiences of harassment. Therefore, it is necessary to take an intersectional approach and to consider gendered experiences interrelated with varying degrees of class, race, sexuality and other systems of oppression and privilege (Bilge, 2010; Carastathis, 2014; Hill Collins, 1986; Hooks, 1981).

This draws attention to the importance of being transparent with regard to who is speaking in this research: whose experiences are being represented, and whose are not. It is worth noting here that pseudonyms are used throughout this book when referring to women's stories. Participants were between the age of 22 and 45. Twenty-four of the women were white, three were of Asian descent and two defined themselves as mixed race; twenty-three were British whilst six identified as non-British nationals; three identified as gay, two as bisexual and twenty-three as heterosexual. Whilst the study called for anyone who identified as a woman, all participants were cis women. Three women discussed having disabilities that impacted on their use of the Underground. As such, it perhaps goes without saying (but will be said anyway!) that the experiences presented in this book should not be considered as representative of how 'all women' perceive and react to sexual harassment. The class and age structure are also recognised as possible limitations of this study. The sample presented in this book mirrors TfL data that show the demographic of those who report experiencing sexual harassment on London public transport. The 2016 TfL Safety and Security report showed that women aged 16–34 were most likely to experience unwanted sexual behaviour on public transport. However, there is literature that suggests *underreporting* of sexual violence is more prevalent amongst the elderly (Bows & Westmarland, 2017), as well as women who are black and ethnic minority (Catalano et al., 2009), and migrant women (Rahmanipour et al., 2019). Therefore, the diversity in this study is limited, and taking a purposive intersectional approach to sampling participants is recommended for future research in order to forefront voices of women who embody a double-minority and potentially experience higher levels of vulnerability and are less likely to report to authorities.

Ethical Considerations

There are significant ethical concerns that must be considered when researching any form of gender-based violence. Recalling incidents of sexual harassment is potentially traumatising and painful for participants. Therefore, interviews were carried out within an ethical praxis relevant for researching sensitive issues, including establishing a lessened hierarchical form of interaction, prioritising the concern for the emotional well-being and rights of participants, and ensuring appropriate levels of anonymity to those taking part in the research (Carroll, 2012). This included emphasising informed consent, confidentiality and anonymity, the right to withdraw and taking a sensitive and flexible approach to interviews. There has been much methodological attention given to how best research sexual violence in an ethical manner. Interview methodology has been used in the field of violence against women since the 1980s and face-to-face semi-structured interviews were used by some of the early studies (Dobash & Dobash, 1979; Kelly, 1988). Campbell et al. (2009) offer useful guidelines in their article 'Training Interviewers for Research on Sexual Violence: A Qualitative Study of Rape Survivors' Recommendations for Interview Practice'. Though my research focusses on sexual harassment, there are numerous points that I found useful to consider in my own research when approaching interviews. The principles they highlight include: the emotional well-being of the participant always being the paramount concern; giving participants time to tell their story with open-ended questions; showing patience and respect as stories unfold; engaging in a dialogue and encouraging participants to ask questions; and finally, to be warm, compassionate and understanding (Campbell et al., 2009, p. 601).

Wolf (1996) discusses 'intersubjectivity' in interviews, when the researcher shares their own experiences with participants. The researcher relating their own experiences may create an environment that encourages sharing and an open dialogue, in comparison to a forced and unnatural format of question and response (Wolf, 1996). Oakley (1981, p. 49) describes this as 'reciprocity' and argues that intimacy and rapport between the interviewer and interviewee cannot be achieved without it. Also, as highlighted by Carroll (2012, p. 548), a common technique used to build rapport and trust is for the researcher to disclose personal experiences. Many of the interviews in this research involved what Oakley (1981) describes as being 'asked back' by research participants. When this happened, I engaged and answered honestly. Often, I was asked about my own experience(s) of harassment on the Underground or in general; why I decided to do this research and what I had found from interviews so far. Furthermore, several participants said how, as no one had asked them about this experience before, getting to finally speak about it made the interview itself feel cathartic or 'like therapy'. Between us, we created a space where we could safely unwrap these neglected yet impactful experiences.

Researcher Reflexivity and Liminality

> *I realise that when I'm riding on the tube, I'm starting to picture the women I've interviewed and their stories of sexual harassment. And looking at the women around me, wondering if they all have their own experiences too.* (Fieldnotes, 15 December 2016)

Early on when I started this research, I became aware of the impossibility of a clear distinction between active research time and formal data collection, and everyday life/leisure time away from the research. Rather than flitting between the dualistic positions of researcher–participant, listener–story-teller, observer–observed, and 'working'– 'not working', a new liminal space opened up where I occupied these positions simultaneously. It was here that I existed for the duration of the research, and on reflection, significantly moulded the theoretical framework I adopted to make sense of women's experiences on the Tube.

I only realised this due to the reflexive diary I kept throughout the research process, snippets of which are incorporated throughout the book. Feminist social scientists have drawn attention to the importance of reflexivity in research (Gelsthorpe & Morris, 1990) and feminist research principles have long recognised that research can never be entirely 'objective' or 'hygienic' (Oakley, 1981). Therefore, whilst not an exclusively feminist practice, reflexivity is regarded as a key theme of feminist research (DeVault, 1996; Ramazanoglu & Holland, 2002). Anderson (2006) describes reflexivity as 'self-conscious introspection' that is guided by the desire to better understand the self and others through the process of examining one's own perceptions and actions. My reflexive journals were separate notebooks to my observational fieldnotes. I wrote how the city, and the Underground made me feel; how I felt before and after every interview and informal conversation; and how I was feeling about the research process as a whole. Keeping a self-reflective journal facilitated reflexivity throughout the research process, and indeed, as Ortlipp (2008) anticipates, revealed to me presuppositions and assumptions I held around the occurrence and impact of sexual violence on public transport. Thus, I was able to avoid moulding other's experiences to fit my expectations/subconscious hypotheses.

As considered above, my reflexive journal also made me aware that I was occupying a liminal state for much of the research process. There was no seamless divide between being a researcher, participant or neither of these. Rather, the boundaries were blurred and leaky. I found myself submerged in the research and struggled (not for lack of trying) to find the off switch. Firstly, I experienced this through the accidental occurrence of 'informal' or 'ethnographic' interviews. Whether at a bar with friends, on a date with a Tinder stranger, or on a weekend away for a hen-do, I regularly found myself drawn into conversations in which people shared their own experiences or those of anonymous friends. It seemed that in a small way, word spread amongst my social circles that I was studying sexual harassment on public transport, and people had stories to share. Close friends, friends of friends, colleagues and relative strangers shared sometimes forgotten incidents, both of their own and people they knew. When small talk turned to 'What do you do for work?', my response ('I'm researching sexual harassment on the Tube') was often met with 'Oh, wow yeah, something like that happened to me/my friend/partner/sister'. Like many incidents of 'low level' sexual harassment, they stayed hidden away, embedded and normalised in the fabric of women's lives, revealed only when prompted by a very specific topic of conversation. Being privy to all these anecdotal stories was unexpected and added a certain depth to the research and my own understanding of the scope and everyday conceptualisation of the issue. However, it also meant that I felt I should be 'on' as a researcher at times when I didn't feel mentally or emotionally able to 'hold' people's stories. I was becoming hypersensitive and vigilant to behaviours I would normally shrug off. After experiencing two explicit incidents of verbal sexual harassment in the same day, I wrote this in my reflexive journal the next morning:

I feel … anger towards the city, the streets, my reaction, the people.
I want to stay at home. I still feel angry and these emotions have
made me exhausted. I want as little interaction with people as pos-
sible today, particularly strangers. I feel like the last few days in
London have drained me. Today I want to hide away from the city.
(Excerpt from reflexive journal, 16 December 2016)

My reflexive journal forced me to acknowledge the emotional impact the
research (in its less explicit form) was having on me. A similar blurring of the lines
happened with my observations of the London Underground. 'Formal' observations took place over a 9-month period and totalled approximately 200 hours,
and are arguably what categorises this research as ethnographic, or more specifically an urban ethnography, an approach that can 'convey the inner life and tex-
ture of the diverse social enclaves and personal circumstances of urban societies'
(Jackson, 1985, p. 157). Urban ethnographies recognise the importance of understanding the everyday context of the city through the immersion of the researcher
into the urban setting (Dunier et al., 2014). The primary aim of these observations was to understand and record the nature (both physical and social) of the
space of the Underground, to immerse myself in its rhythms and regulations, in
order to contextualise experiences of sexual harassment in the space. Fieldnotes
were kept in the form of writing, sketches and photographs, and I also kept notes
in my reflexive diary throughout the process in order to keep track of the changes
and developments in my own perceptions of the city and the Underground. These
observations were intrinsically important to the research process. In the beginning, when everything was new, my fieldnotes were plentiful and detailed – the
Underground and its quirks were visible and fascinating to me. Every journey
on the Tube became an ethnographic observation. How was I supposed to stop
watching, stop observing, when there was so much to see? Travel across the city to
see friends became data, commuting to work became data. However, after a few
months, this shifted and observing became challenging as I felt myself become
immersed in the city and its rhythms. In my reflexive journal I wrote:

Doing observations has become difficult because now everything
seems so normal and mundane. On my regular routes I'm on
auto-pilot- I travel around the network with ease and don't have
to think before I move. I've moulded into the city, its tempo and
pace, dancing in a very disciplined way with everyone around me.

I shifted from being a constantly alert observer, to being too immersed to
be able to actively observe – everything was normal and boring! Yet again, on
reflection, the experience of becoming and embodying the rhythms of the Underground contributed to the unique theoretical framework applied in this book.
Despite finding all these blurred lines difficult to navigate at times, the 'messiness'
of this methodological approach opened conceptual and theoretical avenues. Perhaps then, liminal *state* is a more appropriate expression than space, as it was in

the epistemological *state* I occupied here, this betwixt, messy, intangible arena, where the personal and academic collided.

Book Outline

Incidents of sexual harassment are not static and contained in a single moment. They are mobile and fluid: they are anticipated, lurking in the background as a possibility before they even happen, part of women's psyche and understanding of the world; they are viscerally experienced in an embodied, sensorial way that interrupts, disturbs and demands immediate attention and safety work (Vera-Gray, 2018); they are remembered as feelings of unease, fear or anger lingering long after his hands have left your body, taking the form of a memory that must be redefined and renegotiated, ignored and resisted in order to retain access and freedom to public space.

Using a mobilities framework, this book aims to tell the stories of sexual harassment on the London Underground not as a single, exceptional moment but as part of women's wider urban experiences and movements through public life. The way this book is structured attempts to mirror and portray this. As such, the chapters that follow this one take such an approach: the before, the during and the after. Before this, two chapters are dedicated to the theoretical and conceptual underpinnings that are employed to make sense of women's experiences. **Chapter 2** focusses on our past and current understandings of sexual harassment as a form of gender-based violence and examines sociological theorisations of the issue, with a focus on feminist perspectives. I begin by exploring the varying definitions of sexual harassment over time paying particular attention to how these types of behaviour are understood across contexts, including organisational settings and workplaces, and public spaces like the streets. I will finish the chapter by exploring how the issue has been understood in transport settings thus far, acknowledging the developments and limitations of existing theorisations. This paves the way for the following chapter, that argues for the application of a new lens on an 'old' issue.

Chapter 3 introduces the conceptual framework that I use throughout the rest of the book. Taking a mobilities perspective and focussing on space, temporalities and rhythm, I use this framework to develop our understanding of the way in which sexual harassment is feared and anticipated, experienced, negotiated and remembered in the complex setting of public transport. It problematises the way in which these experiences are often viewed as static and contained (both literally and figuratively), despite happening on the move and blurring time-space boundaries. Applying this framework to women's empirical accounts that are presented in subsequent chapters offers a deeper and more nuanced understanding of the before, during and after of a specific incident of sexual harassment.

Chapter 4 draws on empirical data from women's stories as we start on the 'journey' of experiences of sexual harassment. This chapter focusses on the 'before', as I present women's accounts of everyday life *moving* around London and participating in the rhythmic ensemble of the city. It demonstrates how the city remains a gendered environment that induces both fear and freedom and contextualises the (physical and mental) landscape in which incidents of sexual harassment occur. I will draw on theoretical approaches relating to the emergence of urban modernity in order to contextualise how the social, spatial and temporal conditions in the historical metropolis led to the advent of new sociabilities and modes of being in public life that still influence interactions today. Acknowledging that this remains gendered, I call on the literary character of the *flâneur* to critically analyse women's past and present mobilities in the city. I simultaneously incorporate Lefebvre's concept of rhythm to illustrate how the anticipation and expectation of sexual harassment impacts on women's mobilities so intimately that it constitutes their normative urban rhythms. By exploring women's wider lives in the context of movement and mobilities in the city, this chapter demonstrates the gendered nature of everyday life in the urban environment, including how the anticipation and perceived risk of sexual harassment are experienced and negotiated as an omnipresent possibility.

Chapter 5 focusses on the 'during', the actual corporeal experiences of sexual harassment on the London Underground. I explore these 'moments' in detail, the nitty gritty complexity of these experiences that often hold vulnerability, fear, resistance, anger and ambivalence all at once. As considered above, this complexity can be lost in quantitative work, to the detriment of a nuanced understanding of sexual harassment. In the vein of this book, I continue to explore and understand these moments through the lens of mobility, again operationalising Lefebvre's *rhythmanalysis* in order to draw out key conceptual observations that are specific to how sexual harassment manifests in a public transport environment. Using a mobilities framework, this chapter connects incidents of sexual harassment to general time-space structures of the city and the transport network, illustrating how the various rhythms come together to produce a circumstance where harassment is perpetrated and experienced in a particular way. The framework illustrates how harassment is, in part spatially implicated, facilitated or hindered by the spaces and paces of the city.

Chapter 6 focusses on what happens 'after' the incident of sexual harassment. It explores the impact that the memory of an encounter has on women and their mobilities in the city over time. By employing 'memory' as a sociological concept in order to link space, time and women's embodied experiences, this chapter aims to understand the negotiations that women undertake in order to 'deal with' the incidents of sexual harassment and claim back their mobility and freedom. It pays attention to how the impact is not static, but rather shifts and morphs over time and space. Importantly this analysis moves beyond simply discussing women's fear and vulnerability and makes space for a consideration of how sexual harassment on public transport is negotiated and resisted, and how the experiences or memories are also suppressed and can, at times, act to embolden women in their urban mobilities. Using the conceptual framework structured around mobilities, space and time this chapter offers a unique analysis of the impact of sexual harassment in a transport environment.

Chapter 7 draws this book to a close by returning to the overarching goal of this book – to understand women's experiences of sexual harassment on the London Underground. It brings together the key findings from each chapter. At its core, this book is about deepening and expanding our understanding of sexual harassment on public transport. However, by following the continuous thread of gendered mobilities, we can depart from expected lines of enquiry, broadening our focus to conjoin seemingly disparate conceptual and theoretical approaches and draw out the nuances of these experiences. I also hope this book advocates for why we must not neglect the analysis of the spaces in which these experiences play out. As any ethnographer would contend, we simply cannot claim to understand social interactions without engaging with the cultures and spaces in which they occur and incorporating this into our analyses. So much is revealed through intimate observation of the seemingly mundane – an empty train carriage, the space between strangers, and the invisible rhythms that regulate and play out through our corporeal bodies. This is where we must look to further our enquiries and honour the complexity of these experiences. Along a similar vein, I hope this book demonstrates the continued need to offer space to women's subjective and experiential stories as a form of rich empirical qualitative data. Many of the women I spoke to said they had never been asked about these experiences before and weren't sure if they'd 'remember much' or 'be of any use'. On my side, I expected simplicity, a story along the lines of: a man groped me, I was scared and I never wanted to use the Tube again. Oddly, I expected this despite my own experiences not following this script. And indeed, for most women I spoke to, this was far from the truth. Yes, there was fear, but also guilt, anger, and often, a sense of ambivalence. This does not make the perpetration of these incidents any less serious, but it does reveal the nuance and complexity present in experiences of victimisation and helps us to better understand them, women's reactions to them, and the impact they have.

Chapter 2

Everyday, Everywhere: Theorising Sexual Harassment

Abstract

This chapter delves into our past and current understandings of sexual harassment as a form of gender-based violence and examines sociological theorisations of the issue, with a focus on feminist perspectives. I begin by exploring the varying definitions of sexual harassment over time, paying particular attention to how these types of behaviour are understood across contexts, including organisational settings and workplaces, and public spaces like the streets. I will finish the chapter by exploring how the issue has been understood in transport settings thus far, acknowledging the developments and limitations of existing theorisations. This paves the way for the following chapter, that argues for the application of a new lens on an 'old' issue.

Keywords: Sexual harassment; public space; public transport; London Underground; gender-based violence

It happens everywhere. It doesn't change how I view transport in London because these things are so widespread it happens every-where. That's not cool, but these things are so imbedded into me, I'm so used to them I don't even bat an eyelid at being afraid. (Ally)

It's not always scary when it happens. But it's always annoying. (Kady)

They all blur in to one, it's just something that happens, isn't it? (Eliza)

Mind the Gender Gap: A Mobilities Perspective of Sexual Harassment on the London Underground, 21–37

doi:10.1108/978-1-83753-026-720241002

Whilst the focus of this book is exploring the nuances of how sexual harassment happens within a specific space, I will take the time here to situate these behaviours in broader societal understandings of gender-based violence. Whilst feminists and activist groups have long called for recognition of the prevalence and dangers of sexual harassment, over recent years it has become increasingly visible in public discourse as an endemic societal issue, perpetrated by men against women across different environments (Cuenca-Piqueras et al., 2023). Sexual harassment in its various forms has been recognised as one the most prevalent manifestations of gender-based violence (Bradbury-Jones et al., 2019). This pertains to the socio-cultural model, which is arguably the hegemonic approach to understanding sexual harassment. In simple terms, this theorisation situates sexual harassment as a product of a patriarchal society. It positions sexual harassment and other forms of gender-based violence both as a consequence of a culture that legitimises unequal power dynamics and social standing between men and women, and an act that is perpetrated to maintain this power differential. It exists on a continuum (Kelly, 1987) of behaviours perpetrated by men against women in order to dominate and control. In the past, its prevalence has rendered this kind of behaviour normalised and its harms concealed. Research shows that from a young age, girls 'come up against the wall of patriarchy' (Gilligan, 1990) and learn to perceive and negotiate sexually harassing behaviour as a normal part of everyday life (Fineran & Bennet, 1999; Hlavka, 2014). A socio-cultural theoretical model underpins my academic leaning, as well as matching up with how many of the women in this book understood sexual harassment in a wider context.

Whilst the 'everydayness' of sexual violence runs as an undercurrent to women's lives, episodic spikes in media, public and academic interest often occur in the wake of high-profile incidents. A recent example of this is the Harvey Weinstein scandal and the subsequent growth of the #MeToo movement. In October 2017, the New York Times published a story detailing decades of allegations of sexual harassment against Hollywood mogul Harvey Weinstein. To date, over 80 women have shared experiences of sexual violence they suffered at the hands of the American film producer. Weinstein's accusers gave traction to the #MeToo movement as it is widely known today. Founded by activist Tarana Burke in 2006, 'me too' began as a movement to help Black girls and women show support and discuss their experiences of sexual violence (Boyd & McEwan, 2002). When actress Alyssa Milano called for her followers to share their 'me too' experiences of sexual harassment, it quickly transformed into the hashtag and accompanying viral movement that demonstrated the pervasiveness and magnitude of sexual harassment and assault in the entertainment industry and beyond. The hashtag and its variations caused shockwaves around the globe, with millions of women sharing their stories of harassment and abuse, often for the first time. Sexual harassment and sexual misconduct more broadly became a mainstream talking point.

In 2021, sexual violence in public space made national headlines in the UK. On 3 March, 33-year-old Sarah Everard was kidnapped in London by Wayne

Couzens, a serving Metropolitan Police officer, as she walked home from a friend's house in Clapham. Couzens was later charged with kidnap, rape and murder. The case drew significant media attention and reignited discussions about sexual violence and, more specifically, women's fear and safety in public space. Whilst Sarah's case attracted the media spotlight, it was not an isolated incident or 'unimaginable horror'. For most women, this is *exactly* what they imagine as the 'worst case scenario' when navigating interactions with strange men in public space, and what their plans, energy and safety work are attempting to prevent. This was made visible from the ripple effect and outpouring of everyday stories in the wake of Sarah's murder. For months, the public outrage and distress were palpable, as millions of women's stories reverberated in everyday conversation and around social media with the prolific use of hashtags such as #TextMeWhenYouGetHome, #NotAllMenButAllWomen and the resurgence of #MeToo, #ReclaimTheStreets and #ReclaimTheNight. Several months after Sarah's murder, Sabina Nessa, a 28-year-old teacher, was murdered by Koci Selamaj in a park in South-East London. Unsurprisingly, public commentary drew parallels between the analogous attacks, prompting the reignition of discussions around male violence against women in public space (Bleakley, 2023).

In public transport specifically, the occurrence of sexual harassment and violence has also garnered media attention and community action around the world. In 2012, the gang rape and murder of Jyoti Singh on a bus in New Delhi, India, shook the news on a global scale, raising questions about women's ability to be safe in public spaces and leading to thousands of people across India marching to call for an end to sexual violence and demanding that the government take action. It also prompted amendments to Indian criminal laws around rape and sexual violence (Rajan et al., 2022). In a different vein, conversation was ignited on the back of a 2020 episode of the popular Netflix show 'Sex Education'. Based on the show's creator's own experience, the storyline begins with a much-loved character, Aimee, riding the bus to school when a man masturbates on her leg. Despite speaking out, no one steps in to help her. The impact of the assault threads through subsequent episodes and seasons as the show takes us on a journey where Aimee grapples with how to navigate her experience. We follow her attempts to shrug it off as no big deal, whilst also walking to school to avoid getting on the bus again, imagining seeing the man's face, struggling to be intimate with her partner, and blaming herself for the man's behaviour. Aimee eventually tells her friends about the incident, who then encourage her to report the assault and share their own stories. The episode struck a chord with women around the world, and received significant attention as the show was highly praised across social media for its nuanced representation and shedding light on the issue of sexual assault on public transport.

Though sexual violence on the London transport network is often peppered in the national media, in late 2023 it hit the headlines. On 7 December, an electrical fault caused service disruption to the Underground's Elizabeth line, halting carriages to a standstill for hours and plunging them into darkness. It transpired that during the chaos, there was an arrest due to unwanted sexual touching (The Standard, 2023b). Another high-profile incident came to light after the conviction of a man who, in 2020, sexually assaulted and raped a sleeping woman in view of other passengers on a busy morning Tube service. A significant amount of public outrage caused by these events was targeted towards other passengers – the bystanders who did not intervene. One media article claimed those who do nothing are 'failing Londoners' (The Standard, 2023a).

This increase in awareness of the risk of male violence that women are forced to navigate in public spaces has led to various policies and spatial interventions around the globe. Tokyo, which became infamous for its overcrowded trains and 'endemic groping', introduced women-only carriages in 2005. Perth, Australia, introduced female-only parking spaces, something that already exists in Germany and Switzerland. Highly populated cities in Egypt, Iran, Indonesia, India, Brazil, Mexico, Malaysia and the UAE have all implemented some form of women-only transport (Horii & Burgess, 2012). The idea has also been floated in the UK. Whilst feminist groups around the world highlight that this method endorses segregation and is essentially regressive for gender equality (Gekoski et al., 2015), it signifies the risk of gendered violence in public transport that women around the world experience as a part of everyday life. In the UK, high profile incidents of violence have led to government and organisational interventions, including the 2018 Parliamentary Inquiry into the sexual harassment of women and girls in public spaces, which included a focus on transport environments. In the wake of Sarah Everard's murder, the government increased funding to the 'Safer Streets' campaign which largely focusses on making public spaces less hostile to women. In recent years, Transport for London (TfL) and British Transport Police (BTP) have pushed high profile and priority campaigns (detailed below) that focus on combatting unwanted sexual attention on the London Underground. Amid this bubbling public and political interest, where sexual violence and harassment in transport are gaining recognition as an issue that needs significant attention, it is imperative that we fully understand these experiences. We need to scrutinise and dismantle 'taken for granted' understandings of sexual harassment, and forefront women's in-depth stories that portray the way in which sexual harassment is perpetrated and experienced, and the way in which it impacts women's mobilities and every day life.

After a brief note on definitions of 'sexual harassment' and my choice to use the term for this book, this chapter traces the development of conceptualisations of sexual harassment across different social spaces. I examine the various and specific features of how sexually harassing behaviours manifest in different contexts, from workplace and organisational settings to public space and public transport and examine what we know so far about how this behaviour is perpetrated on the London Underground. Doing this allows us to identify how modes of committing sexual harassment mutate and shift depending on the socio-spatial nexus in which it occurs. This also exposes the limitations in the existing theorisations of sexual harassment 'on the move' and reveals the subsequent gap in knowledge that this book aims to address.

'I'm Not Sure if This Even Counts': Defining Sexual Harassment

> *I think a big problem is that we didn't have a language for it ... for a long time it's been missing in our dialogue, so how do you describe what happened to you? So many of these little incidents become invalidated or internalised.* (Janice)

> *I have a very broad ranging view of what sexual harassment is. So much of it is micro aggressive shit ... ultimately, it's anything where one person makes another uncomfortable in a way that is not platonic. And that encompasses a huge range of stuff. So, I don't think there's a one size fits all definition of sexual harassment.* (Laya)

Before examining how sexual harassment manifests across difference spaces, it is important to note the terminology chosen for this book, as it has methodological and conceptual implications. In the 1970s, feminist scholars and activists brought to public attention the importance of naming and legally addressing sexually harassing behaviour in workplace settings (Brownmiller, 1975; Farley, 1978; MacKinnon, 1979; Rowe, 1974). Whilst 'sexual harassment' has existed as a term in everyday language ever since, due to the origins of the term, it has often referred to behaviour in traditionally structured organisational environments. Consequently, sexual harassment was often viewed with limited scope to mean unwanted sexual relations imposed by superiors on subordinates at work (MacKinnon & Siegel, 2004). Of course, this restrictive understanding of the term negates identifying sexually harassing behaviours that occur in public space and operate within a differing social power dynamic.

Researchers exploring the issue have highlighted the difficulties in appropriately labelling sexual harassing behaviour in public space (Vera-Gray, 2016) and the concurrent struggle in unearthing what to many women, is perceived as an everyday experience. Sexual harassment is being increasingly described as unwelcome or unwanted sexual attention, particularly within organisational settings (the London Underground included; this is the terminology used by both TfL and the BTP) (Gekoski et al., 2015; Solymosi et al., 2017). However, many of the experiences of public harassment including on transport, are difficult to define as explicitly sexualised in nature [e.g. a stranger silently taking hold of your hand, or an aggressive (non-sexual) verbal assault]. Feminist academics have sought to combat this limitation in reference to these behaviours more broadly. One term I find particularly useful is 'men's stranger intrusions' (Vera-Gray, 2016). With the use of this term, Vera-Gray addresses the lack of gendering in commonly used terminology, and the risk of excluding experiences that are not overtly 'sexual'. This term is accurate for many of the behaviours being perpetrated on the London Underground. Firstly, all the incidents were committed by men who were strangers to the victims. And secondly, whilst only around half were overtly sexual (whether in terms of groping/flashing/verbal comments), all were understood as intrusions – indeed, many women saw these experiences as *particularly* intrusive or disruptive in comparison to similar experiences in other spaces. This was because: (a) they happened on the move, so they were forced to 'deal' with them whilst trying to get somewhere else; and (b) they occurred in a space where this behaviour was so unexpected and out of place (say, in comparison to a bar or nightclub) – often intruding not just in the moment but on their ontological sense of safety in a space they felt was theirs to occupy without the risk of invasion. Similarly, the term 'gender-based harassment' is arguably a more accurate term, as women are often targets of these intrusions because of their gender, rather than for sexual 'purposes' or gain (i.e. flirtation), as 'sexual harassment' may imply.

Another consideration was consistently using one of the two wider umbrella terms, 'gender-based violence' or 'sexual violence', that would then incorporate sexual harassment into their domain. However, I was concerned that by using this language in the call for participants, I would only connect with women who had experienced more physically intrusive forms of sexual violence such as rape or physical assault. Whilst in the social sciences conceptualisations of violence have moved beyond the physical and interpersonal to incorporate a broader understanding of harm, in everyday discourse violence is still often perceived only as an action that inflicts physical pain. Because of this, I was concerned that women who had experienced the more 'everyday' and 'normalised' behaviours (such as intense leering, catcalling, even non-painful groping) would not respond to the call. This proved to be a relevant concern. There were several women who initially responded tentatively to the call for participants, unsure whether their experience 'counted as sexual harassment' or was 'bad enough', when in fact, legally it would be considered sexual assault.

> I knew it was wrong and I knew what I was seeing was completely wrong but I think at the time I wouldn't have put it down as sexual harassment, I would have just put it down to this guy being a creep but I wouldn't have thought wait, this is sexual harassment. (Carla)

> I had a google before I came, to see if I fell into the spectrum ..., you're in a public space, is it someone you know, someone you don't know, that all plays into it and a lot to do with the space and how you feel. (Tara)

> Even though I knew I felt uncomfortable and I didn't like it, I wouldn't have framed it as sexual harassment. (Emmy)

> It's difficult because the occasions I've experienced it on public transport, only one of these was I actually touched. The other two they sat opposite me touching themselves ... so I don't know if it counts, but I'm still being violated. (Ally)

Many of the experiences described in this book are void of acute physical pain, but rather are suffused with immediate and long-lasting discomfort and unease. I wanted to make sure to catch these experiences. Furthermore, whilst 'sexual harassment' may hold the same connotations (and therefore the same limitations) as 'unwanted sexual attention', I contend that the term occupies a more tangible and established space in our lexicon and psyche, and it is with this rationale that I used the term sexual harassment during the research process. As such, it felt important to use the same terminology in the book, as this is how the participants engaged with and related to the research. The term 'sexual harassment' then has been used for its prominence in our everyday comprehension of a complex issue, as the 'hook', to engage both participants in the research and readers of this book.

Alongside murky language and the normalisation of behaviour, another way that experiences of sexual harassment are rendered invisible or difficult to define, is the complex reality of women's multifaceted identities. Intersectionality highlights that individuals experience overlapping forms of discrimination based on multiple aspects of their identity (Crenshaw, 1989). An intersectional approach to understanding sexual harassment is essential. Also referred to as a 'multidimensional model' in organisational settings (Fitzgerald & Buchanan, 2008), it draws attention to the complex ways in which various forms of discrimination can intersect to shape and compound experiences of harassment. Most explicitly, an intersectional approach highlights how sexism and racism compound to create different experiences of oppression (Crenshaw, 1989). For example, misogynoir refers to anti-Black racist misogyny that Black women experience (Bailey & Trudy, 2018) and addresses the racialised nuance that mainstream feminism was overlooking when speaking to experiences of misogyny. Similarly, intersectionality draws attention to (in this instance) how LGBTQ+ individuals, people from marginalised socio-economic backgrounds and people with disabilities may experience sexual harassment differently to cis, heterosexual, white, middle-class, able-bodied women – on whose experiences research is often focussed. Fogg-Davis (2006) considers this in his work on the victimisation of Black lesbians, claiming the importance of recognising both civic behaviours and how they interact with structural inequalities (such as colonialism and heterosexism).

Social climate is often significant as to why peaks in harassment against marginalised groups occur, and how experiences of sexual harassment become more explicitly intertwined with racist and xenophobic tones. For example, Mason-Bish and Zempi's (2018) work 'Misogyny, Racism, and Islamophobia: Street Harassment at the Intersections' explored veiled Muslim women's experiences of harassment in public space, highlighting how in a socio-political climate rife with islamophobia and sexism, women are targeted for their gender, religion and culture. During the COVID-19 pandemic racially motivated harassment and public hate crimes against Asian communities increased (Karandikar et al., 2024), and a gendered analysis of this showed that Asian women compromised two-thirds of those reporting verbal and physical assault. Unless made explicit through aggressive sexist language, this overlapping of discrimination can shroud women's experiences in confusion as to whether they have been explicitly targeted because of their gender or their religion/ethnicity/disability and as such, this impacts on whether it is defined and acknowledged as sexual harassment. Intersectionality ensures that we acknowledge that gender is not the only factor that implicates or motivates these experiences. Whilst the experiences I analyse in this book are situated in the 'microcosm' of the London Underground, they are still located within and impacted by the broader context of social, political and economic dynamics 'above ground' that fluctuate and insidiously impact on women's lives. Furthermore, they are often only one part of the tapestry of women's understandings and experiences of sexual violence, and therefore, it is important to review how other experiences manifest in different contexts, setting the scene that allows us to discern what is different and particular about public transport.

Sexual Harassment in Organisational Settings

As noted briefly above, sexual harassment was originally conceptualised in feminist studies that focussed on naming sexually harassing behaviours in the workplace (MacKinnon, 1979). The goal was primarily to identify and label these widely normalised interactions so they could be dealt with through official organisational and legal channels. Conceptions of sexual harassment within the workplace follow that it is perpetrated as an exertion and abuse of power, rather than as an act of sexual desire (MacKinnon, 1979). Cortina and Areguin (2021) contend that, reframed as gendered harassment, the root of this behaviour is contempt, and the goal to intimidate and exclude from the workplace rather than to engage in sexual activity. A structural power analysis contends that sexual harassment in this context is behaviour that abuses hierarchical organisational structures and most commonly takes the form of men in positions of economic power taking advantage of and exploiting relationships with women in less powerful positions, often without fear of reprisal. However, contrary to this being the exclusive dynamic, research has shown how co-workers holding similar organisational power were often reported to commit harassing behaviours (Brant & Too, 1994), and Rospenda et al. (1998) theorise 'contrapower sexual harassment', to explain when the target of harassment has greater organisational power than the harasser. At times, this can act to reflect intersectional influences of gender, race and class on power dynamics in a workplace setting. It also shows how broader gendered power differentials infiltrate and often override organisational power dynamics.

Whilst internal sexual harassment is considered to be the most common form of workplace sexual harassment, women also experience sexually harassing behaviour from male customers. This is reported to be particularly prevalent for those in customer service positions, particularly in nighttime economy settings (Green, 2022). Other organisational settings with complex power dynamics that are important to consider include higher educational settings. Bondestam and Lundqvist (2020) argue that these constitute an accumulation of precarious working conditions, hierarchical structure, toxic academic masculinities, a culture of silence and a lack of active leadership as well as a normalisation of gender-based violence, that combine to enable an epidemic of sexual harassment.

Across these organisational contexts, hostile or overtly sexist environments can be fostered by managers and colleagues, permitting space for the occurrence of intimidating conduct and subsequent silence. Hand and Sanchez (2000) describe this form of unwelcome sexual behaviour as often including lewd comments, circulating rumours, and using demeaning language that interrupts a person's ability to do their job. In masculinised environments and traditionally male dominated occupations women were more likely to be touched or grabbed and be subjected to sexualised jokes (Gruber, 1998). Here, it is useful to consider how sexual harassment can also constitute a public performance and affirmation of masculinity (Connell, 1995). Within these settings, peer harassment often reflects performances of hegemonic masculinity for other men, displaying compulsory heterosexuality and acting as a form of 'homosocial bonding' (Kimmel, 2008) through 'girl watching' (Quinn, 2002), where men sexually evaluate women in the company of other men. These more normalised or 'everyday' forms of harassment also constitute an atmosphere in which sexual harassment and violence in more explicit terms can occur, in the form of unwanted sexual advances and coercive behaviours, such as pressure for sexual favours as a condition of employment.

This collusion of organisational structures and atmospheres perpetuates a climate of silence, as victims fear revicitimisation, inaction, job loss or damage to their careers (Spiliopoulou & Witcomb, 2023). Krasas and Henson (1997, p. 229) suggest there is a response matrix or continuum with regard to reactions to sexual harassment in the workplace, including four major types: avoidance, diffusion, negotiation and confrontation. For example, in their research on temporary workers they observed that women in insecure and vulnerable employment learnt to tolerate sexual harassment by shifting their 'anger boundaries'. Again, context is significant as to how women experienced and responded to such behaviour. As Schneider (1991) considers, women react based on a fear of the depersonalising and humiliating organisational procedures that they have learnt to anticipate if they were to speak out about their experience. In the workplace, sexual harassment is generally perpetrated by men who are known to the victim, and in a setting that is not easy for the victim to detach herself from without serious social and financial repercussions. Intimacy, economic dependency and a conflation of relationships of power are significant as to how sexual harassment is perpetrated and experienced within this context. Whilst these systems are highly flawed, theoretically, within organisational settings, there should be clear avenues and frameworks within which to report. I say this in comparison to street-based public harassment, where a lack of structure often renders these experiences to be considered unreportable. This is important to bear in mind when thinking about the London Underground, which sits as a liminal space that is seemingly public yet is simultaneously managed by stakeholders and governing bodies who control and manage the space and interactions that occur within it, with their own regulations and reporting mechanisms. The identification and naming of sexual harassment in organisational settings paved the way for further understanding the mechanisms of this kind of behaviour and the impact it had on women's participation in the workplace. Yet these conceptualisations are not entirely transferable to other settings, including public spaces, which require their own analysis.

Sexual Harassment in Public Space

As considered in the previous chapter, the acknowledgement that sexual harassment is a predominant and impacting feature of women and girls' existence has become a public policy issue on a global scale. It is now widely documented that women feel disproportionally unsafe in public space, largely due to fears and experiences of sexual violence from men (Fileborn, 2019). 'Lower level' sexual harassment plays a significant role in the production and extent of these fears, acting as a reminder of visibility and vulnerability under the objectifying male gaze (Boyer, 2022). Brooks Gardner (1995) challenged that as a society we have neglected to acknowledge the harms of public harassment, especially heterosexually romanticised public harassment. By this, she means behaviours that are often considered (by men) as harmless and flirtatious, such as wolf-whistling and catcalling – comments or behaviours that are wrapped up and defended as compliments (Di Gennaro & Ritschel, 2019). Again, we can utilise Kelly's (1987) 'continuum of sexual violence', to understand how sexual harassment that is so common it is regarded as 'everyday male behaviour', still acts to instil fear. Sexual harassment is on a continuum of possible events in public space, an interaction that begins when civility amongst strangers is disrupted and ends with the transition to violent assault, rape or murder. As such, the regular occurrence of sexual harassment acts as a constant reminder of the risk of a more severe sexual attack and creates a state of anxiety and unease that women must navigate (Pain, 1991). The gendered norms that underpin this historically are explored in much more detail in Chapter 4, so here I will overview key understandings around its manifestation in contemporary society.

Whilst located against the same social backdrop as occurrences of organisational sexual harassment, there are distinct differences in how it manifests and is experienced 'on the streets' in comparison to in the workplace. Not mitigated or sanctioned by the same organisational power structures, sexual harassment in public space has its own key features. Bowman (1993, p. 523) highlights these as: (1) the targets of street harassment are female; (2) the harassers are male; (3) the harassers are unacquainted with their targets; (4) the encounter is face to face; (5) the forum is a public one (in this she includes public transport); and (6) the content of speech, if any, is not intended as public discourse. Sexual harassment in public space is widely considered to include unwelcome physical contact or advances, stalking, lewd gestures and voyeurism, as well as verbal behaviours (Madan & Nalla, 2016). Brooks Gardner (1995) includes scrutiny, exhibitionism, public aid exchanges or greetings with innuendo and romantic overtones and determined following. Pain (1991, p. 421) defined such behaviour as 'unwanted intrusive acts perpetrated by men against women, including staring, touching and comments or actions of a sexual nature'. In India, street harassment is often called 'eve teasing' (Dhillon & Bakaya, 2014), and a type of catcalling, sometimes understood by men as a form of gallantry and colloquially called pirópo, is pervasive in Latin America (Bailey, 2017).

Key features of how women experience and perceive incidents of sexual harassment in public space have been identified. According to Bailey (2017), street harassment in the form of remarks is often not understood as explicitly threatening, yet it is a reminder of vulnerability (Tuerkheimer, 1997). As women learn to perceive strange men in public space as potentially dangerous (Hubbard, 2012), increased feelings of fear and vulnerability can reinforce gender inequality through restricting mobility or contribute to what Bowman (1993) terms 'the informal ghettoization of women', acting to 'keep women in their place' (Crouch, 2009, p. 137). Significant theoretical work has also discussed how women perceive such acts as *intrusions* (Bowman, 1993; Vera-Gray, 2016). These intrusions have been seen as problematic to women's freedom in public space and as invasions of women's right to privacy in public (Brooks Gardner, 1995). Swim and Hyers (1999) highlight that women often react to public harassment in a non-confrontational way due to fear of escalation, fear of being perceived as impolite, societal pressure and 'lines' not being crossed by the harasser (in subsequent chapters, we see all of these dynamics play out in women's accounts of harassment on the Tube). Dhillon and Bakaya (2014) state that women's experiences of sexual harassment often include a combination of self-protective strategies and emotional reactions of fear and anger. In public space, women are unable to predict whether male behaviour may escalate (Stanko, 1993; Vera-Gray, 2018), and it is with a 'worst case scenario' in mind that women often respond. Whilst I knew this latently, I became more acutely aware of these negotiations during this research, as I wrote every incident of sexual harassment I experienced across the city in my fieldnotes and reflexive diary. There's one incident I wrote about in particular detail that I'll summarise below.

> After having drinks and dinner with two of my closest friends, I'm walking to the bus stop, cutting off the busy main road down a quiet street lined with trees, whitewashed houses and the intermittent glow cast by dim streetlights. It's a brusque December evening, and the wine buzz mingles with the bite of static wintry air and I smile contentedly, breathing in the city, and pulling my thick coat tightly around me. Down the street, two men appear, turning the corner and walking towards me. My body and brain shift from relaxed to tense. I immediately clock that they're big in stature, they're around my age, maybe early thirties, headphones looped around their necks as they're chatting animatedly. The pavement is wide and they don't seem to be paying me any attention. I feel myself relax. Just as they're passing me, one of them looks at me and says 'Oh my God, you're beautiful' and licks his lips, searing his eyes into me. My mind jolts. Usually, I'd ignore this, particularly given the setting – it might be a pleasant street, but its dark and isolated, and the fact that in the grand scheme of unwanted sexual attention, this was paltry in scale, non-physical, not even aggressive, *almost* passable as an unthreatening 'compliment'. Yet after months of hearing women's stories of this kind of unwanted attention from men, my anger and resentment bubbles to the surface, dances on my tongue and slips from under the

veneer of nonchalance, contorting my face into a sharp frown. I say nothing, but this look is enough to dramatically shift the gears in this interaction. Their pace slows, and one of them loudly asserts 'What the fuck is that about? FUCK you, you should be saying thank you'. My heart vaults, and I turn, quickening my pace as I walk away, an ugly mix of anger and fear metastasising in my stomach.

I'm scared they'll follow me

> *I'm angry I didn't say anything or do more*

I'm scared there's no-one else around

> *I'm angry at their complete disregard for how their behaviour might make me feel*

I'm scared of violence

> *I'm angry at myself for putting myself at risk of violence*

It doesn't have to come close to the 'worst case scenario' to feel threatening, for violence to become easily conceivable, a mere 'wrong move' away. It is this parallel sequence of events that we are often in negotiation with. Laya, a participant in the research, summarised this succinctly:

[…] And you get that transition from oh hey, alright darling, and the moment you deny them what they want it turns into, fucking bitch, you should be thankful someone's looking at you. And that's the flipside to all these types of engagements, we all know it's not a compliment because fucking bitch is right at the back of it.

Like in organisational settings, experiences of sexual harassment in public spaces are widely underreported (Fileborn & O'Neill, 2023). Again, the normalisation of these intrusions from men means they are trivialised, perceived as an expected and unavoidable part of everyday life, with many of these interactions being considered too minor to report (Mellgren et al., 2018). Low levels of reporting are exacerbated by women's perception that they would not be taken seriously by the police (Dhillon & Bakaya, 2014), may be met with victim blaming and inaction (Boutros, 2018), and the awareness of ineffective legal frameworks to reprimand offenders, thus rendering the reporting process both hostile and futile. As a semi-public space, sexual harassment in transport has many similarities to street harassment in how it is perpetrated and experienced. However, the unique spatial, temporal and social nature of public transport accounts for the specific ways in which sexual harassment manifests and is negotiated within this environment.

Sexual Harassment on Public Transport

Situated in a broader gendered critique of urban space (Matrix, 2022), early feminist work focussed on highlighting how transport systems were structured to serve men's everyday requirements. Simultaneously, they emphasised that women often have vastly different travel needs than men (Little, 1994) and as such, the 'gender blind' nature of transport acted to curtail women's access and freedom and excluded them from public spaces. On top of this, they raised awareness of the fear of sexual violence that many women experience when using public transport. Since then, research has continued to show that vulnerable groups, including women, often perceive transport as a space of vulnerability, rather than safety (Loukaitou-Sideris & Fink, 2009). Subsequently, gender has been recognised by transport authorities to impact on travel and has been considered in the designing and implementation of policy. The prevalence of sexual harassment in public transport remains an increasing concern for authorities and I explore this specifically in relation to the London Underground below.

There is a growing body of work uncovering various facets of the phenomenon of unwanted sexual attention in transport, including: the fear of sexual harassment and assault (Carver & Veitch, 2020); the frequency and nature of sexual harassment in transit (Ison et al., 2023; Loukaitou-Sideris & Ceccato, 2020); the phenomenon of underreporting (Solymosi et al., 2017), the impact of sexual harassment on women's future travel (Koskela, 1999) and media reporting of the issue (Mowri & Bailey, 2023). There has also been a growth in work that identifies the harassing behaviours that are prevalent in a transport environment (Valan, 2020). This research has shown that the spaces of public transport are exploited in numerous ways, at varying times of day. One of the most investigated times (both academically and by authorities) is the commuter 'rush hours', congruent with the 9 to 5 working day, where bodies are densely packed together in small spaces. The sort of behaviours that are regularly reported to occur during these times include frotteurism (rubbing the pelvic area or erect penis against a non-consenting person for sexual pleasure) and unwanted sexual touching (Shoukry et al., 2008). In Japan, this widespread groping on carriages is termed 'chikan' (Horii & Burgess, 2012). Chowdhury (2023) discusses this in the context of Tokyo and describes the 'sexual politics of commuter crowds', considering how sexual violence in mass transit environments produces everyday knowledge about the nature of shared mobility. It becomes clear that there is an exploitation of the social dynamics of the space: the overcrowded nature of transport at peak times permits bodily contact and the perpetration of sexual harassment in a particular, embodied way (Neupane & Chesney-Lind, 2014). The necessary proximity to others is exploited in a similar way to the perpetration of sexual assault in crowds at festivals or in a night club (Bows et al., 2024). However, there is more at play here than propinquity, as there are discerning differences in the social atmospheres and norms of these spaces. Festival and night-time economy environs are often socially lubricated with alcohol, drugs and the desire for spontaneous interaction – in these spaces this is also exploited in conjunction with close physical contact (Kavanaugh, 2013). On public transport, despite the 'public' nature of the space, they are commonly highly individualistic and insular, with interactions minimal and sterile, often there in order for the mass of commuters to be able to cope with the urban stimuli and proximity. As previously discussed, this is immediately discernible on the London Underground. In these spaces, it is the apathy, deference or civil inattention (Goffman, 1963) that is exploited, as offenders depend on these hostile social norms to keep victims and bystanders uncertain and silent. Exemptions to this in London could be the late night or 'night Tubes' that often shuttle partygoers across the city. Here, 'romanticised' sexual harassment is rife in the form of strong come-ons and unwanted, persistent 'flirtation' that is often forced to be temporarily endured due to the trapped nature of the carriage moving between stations.

The picture is quite different when looking at 'off peak' travel times, particularly night travel, or more isolated rural settings. It is perhaps these time-spaces that occupy a place in women's psyche as to where more physical sexual violence might occur and where fear lingers heavily in the space between you and the only other person on the carriage. The uneasiness that, hung suspended in the air, jolts suddenly when the man catches your eye and tries to hold your gaze for a moment too long. Again, in these situations, the worst is anticipated and seems plausible. These imaginings are largely facilitated by the isolated space of the transport environment and solidified by the epistemological understanding of the risk of gendered stranger violence. Indeed, it is in these settings that 'more extreme' violent sexual assaults and rape more commonly occur (Ding et al., 2020). As well as these incidents of violence, quiet and solitary spaces of transport often host incidents of flashing and masturbation (UK Parliament, 2018). Of course, some of these behaviours leak across expected time-space dynamics. Behaviours that especially transgress these time categorisations include lewd, sexualised comments, sexual invitations, leering and stalking. Smith and Clarke (2000) consider that other elements of the environment that impact the prevalence of these behaviours include poor surveillance and supervision, and a lack of patrolling on public transport. It is also important to mention the rise of technologically mediated harassment on public transport, the rise of which is congruent to its occurrence in other social spaces (Henry et al., 2020; Salerno-Ferraro et al., 2022). This can be in the form of watching pornography publicly, air dropping offensive or sexual images, up-skirting and other forms of photographing or filming without consent.

Sexual Harassment on the London Underground

Throughout this book, I draw on women's anecdotal, perceptual and experiential understandings of the space of the London Underground. Alongside my own fieldnote excerpts from observations of the space, it is through a tapestry of these descriptions and stories that the 'research environment' will be depicted. As little has been written about sexual harassment on the London Underground (hence the writing of this book) I will briefly overview the work that does exist and then move on to explore how the governing bodies of the London Underground (primarily TfL and BTP) understand sexual harassment, how they have tried to combat it, and what we can learn from their campaigns.

As signalled above, the majority of studies looking at sexual harassment on public transport have been conducted in the global South (see Horii & Burgess, 2012; Lim, 2002; Marcela Quinones, 2020; Mowri & Bailey, 2023; Neupane & Chesney-Lind, 2014; Shoukry et al., 2008). Ding et al. (2020) offer a review of the existing research that looks at the global North, yet these are predominantly focussed on Australia, the USA and Scandinavia. There remains very little written on sexual harassment in UK transport (with the exception of Gekoski et al., 2015 and Solymosi & Newton, 2020) and even less focussing on the London Underground specifically. That which does exist mirrors broader trends in research of sexual harassment, with a focus on understanding prevalence and underreporting (Gekoski et al., 2015). Solymosi et al. (2017) provide a realist evaluation of the effects of the Report It to Stop It (RITSI) campaign (detailed below) on victims' willingness to report unwanted sexual behaviour on the Tube. They found that the 2015 media campaign raised awareness and led to 'waves' of increased reporting. They also signified that the campaign did not increase passengers fear of crime and highlighted the importance of context in motivating reporting behaviour change. In her Ph.D. work, Shola Apena Rogers focusses on offender behaviours and motivations when committing sexual offences on London trains. Interviewing fifteen proactive police officers, five convicted offenders and analysing case records and offender data, she identifies 'the desire to achieve a thrill' and the perception of London transport being an easy place to get away with it, as key motivators for offenders. She also highlights the police's pro-active 'hunting process' for sexual offences. I have explored elsewhere how sexual harassment is policed on the Underground (Lewis, 2023). Focussing on how the BTP pro-actively and reactively manage incidents of unwanted sexual attention, I show how their knowledge of the issue is constructed through a coalition of organisational police culture and technologies. Significantly, the rhythms and sociabilities of the network were implicit in how BTP sought out and located offenders.

Above I discussed the organisational theory of sexual harassment, which focusses on organisational culture and power dynamics to understand incidents of sexual harassment. Whilst this approach is commonly operationalised to understand inter-organisational dynamics of sexual harassment, it is also useful here. As a public—private, or semi-public space, the social behaviours that occur within the London Underground system, are in part, regulated and mitigated by its governing bodies. For a broader context and a deeper understanding of the often-invisible management of the space, I will overview how key stakeholders have given attention to and attempted to curtail sexual harassment on the network through public awareness campaigns. These campaigns have the potential to impact on the perpetration, experience of and reaction to sexual harassment within these spaces.

TfL is the integrated body responsible for the majority of the city's transport system and is one of the largest transport operators in the world. Over the last decade or so TfL has put significant effort into understanding and responding to women's transport needs (Loukaitou-Sideris & Fink, 2009). In 2004, TfL initiated its first *Women's Action Plan for London* entitled 'Expanding Horizons', prompted by the recognition of the differing demands and issues of men and women using the network. Herbel and Gaines (2009, p. 113) described this as 'arguably the most comprehensive effort by a transport operator to respond to the needs of women riders'. This included increasing the percentage of women participating in TfL's labour force; a significant increase in CCTV surveillance; and an inclusion of women's voices in the planning process. In 2014, the TfL Safety and Security annual report revealed that one in ten Londoners experienced 'unwanted sexual behaviour' on public transport, but over 90% of those did not report it to authorities (SPA Future Thinking, 2014). Prompting the need to tackle both the prevalence of sexual harassment and the issue of underreporting, this led to the creation of Project Guardian and its inclusive and successive campaigns that have been implemented on the London Transport Network by TfL and the BTP, alongside other stakeholders, over the last decade.

At its inception, Project Guardian was one of the most comprehensive, multi-method programmes in the world aimed at reducing sexual harassment on public transport (Gekoski et al., 2015). The project pledged to take all reports seriously, to identify perpetrators and held the overall aim of reducing all sexual crime on the trains, Tubes and buses. Project Guardian incorporated a variety of initiatives including: the targeting of 'hotspots', action weeks of officers talking to the public, training packages for BTP and Metropolitan Police officers, community engagement and social media and advertising campaigns (Gekoski et al., 2015). It also trained 2,000 police officers and police community support officers to deal with cases of sexual harassment, who were dedicated to patrol the transport network. Under the umbrella of Project Guardian, there are two key interventions that are particularly important to consider. Report it to Stop it, also know as RITSI, was a 2015 publicity campaign led by TfL and supported by BTP. The campaign was deemed a success in raising public awareness and increasing the reporting of incidents (Solymosi et al., 2017). Launched by TfL, BTP, Metropolitan Police Service and City of London Police in March 2017, Every Report Builds a Picture was the second campaign targeted at encouraging women to come forward and report unwanted sexual behaviour on public transport. It emphasised how reports can be collated in order to identify, arrest and prosecute repeat offenders. It is within the context of these campaigns that the research for this book took place. Since then, there have been numerous successive campaigns focussing on different areas of the issue. In 2022, a campaign was launched that highlighted less explicit behaviours such as 'staring', 'pressing', 'cyber flashing', 'exposing', 'upskirting' and 'catcalling'. The campaign was highly visible, with posters displayed in stations, platforms and carriages (both on the Tube and trains and stations around the country) and received significant media attention. Another campaign was launched in early 2023 that focussed on creating an 'active bystander' culture to support victims and lead to an increase in reporting. Launched by TfL in partnership with Rail Delivery Group, BTP, Metropolitan Police Service and City of London Police, it offered advice on how passengers can look out for each other and safely intervene when witnessing incidents of sexual harassment. In February 2024, a new campaign was launched called 'Your Piece of the Puzzle'. The aim of the campaign is to show the importance of reporting. It uses the real words of victims to show how the information they came forward with led to a serial sex offender being apprehended. Through this campaign, BTP is sharing with the public that they hold extensive knowledge of offences, and that this knowledge is, in part, built from victim reports. They also focus on the fact that many perpetrators commit multiple offences and that multiple reports help to connect the dots and identify repeat offenders (Lewis, 2023).

This chapter has traced how sexual harassment is understood, manifests and is experienced across different contexts. It is vital that sexual harassment on the London Underground is situated in this broader web of established and normalised gender-based violence. This contextualises incidents of sexual harassment on the Underground, showing they are not isolated, but are perpetrated as part of the continuum of various forms of actual and feared violence across time and space. This chapter has followed the developments that show growing academic attention towards sexual harassment in public transport environments. However, I hope I have also demonstrated the need for innovative inquiry and the benefit of qualitative approaches that prioritise women's nuanced and multifaceted stories, and the importance of the development and application of new conceptual frameworks in order to tease out the intricacies of these experiences and expand our knowledge and understanding. The following chapter connects sexual harassment as a form of gender-based violence to a mobilities framework to make sense of women's stories that are presented in subsequent chapters.

Chapter 3

Space, Time and Rhythms: Introducing a Mobilities Framework

Abstract

This chapter introduces the conceptual framework that I use throughout the rest of the book. Taking a mobilities perspective and focussing on space, temporalities and rhythm, I use this framework to develop our understanding of the way in which sexual harassment is feared, anticipated, experienced, negotiated and remembered in the complex setting of public transport. It problematises the way in which these experiences are often viewed as static and contained (both literally and figuratively), despite happening on the move and blurring time–space boundaries. Applying this framework to women's empirical accounts that are presented in subsequent chapters offers a deeper and more nuanced understanding of the before, during and after of a specific incident of sexual harassment.

Keywords: Sexual harassment; public transport; mobilities; rhythmanalysis; space; time

> *Might there be hidden, **secret**, rhythms, hence inaccessible movements and temporalities? No, because there are **no secrets**. Everything knows itself, but not everything says itself, publicises itself. Do not confuse silence with secrets! That which is forbidden from being said, be it external or intimate, produces an obscure, but not a secret, zone.* (Lefebvre, 2004, p. 17)

Mind the Gender Gap: A Mobilities Perspective of Sexual Harassment on the London Underground, 39–50

The order … does not arise from intimacy and connectedness, but rather from some of the very things more often presumed to bring about conflict and violence – transiency, fragmentation, isolation, atomization, and indifference among people. (Baumgartner, 1988, p. 134)

In their review of research that explores sexual crimes in transit in the global North, Ding et al. (2020) show that the few studies that examined the relationship between attributes of the physical and social environment of transit settings and sexual crimes did so using police records, google street view, geographical information systems (GIS) and regression models (Ceccato, 2017; Ceccato & Paz, 2017; Ceccato & Uittenbogaard, 2014) and focussed on the role of environmental factors such as lighting, visibility, seclusion, dirty environments and proximity to alcohol sales or drunk people. A theme that weaves through much existing research is the application of routine activity theory to understand sexual assault on or near transit (Cohen & Felson, 1979; Felson et al., 2021; Lersch & Hart, 2023; Savard, 2018), thus offering solutions located within the realm of situational crime prevention, or crime prevention through environmental design. Though these approaches have been invaluable in linking incidents of sexual harassment with space and time, locating hostile environments, and identifying an axis of vulnerability, they can be limited in their scope. For example, routine activity theory posits that crime happens because of the convergence of a motivated offender, a suitable target, and the absence of a capable guardian. However, on a crowded bus or Tube, there are arguably numerous capable guardians to intervene – and yet sexual harassment is rife. Here, in the husk of the carriage, in the spaces between strangers, the atmosphere is thick and laden with an intangible substance that both constitutes and regulates social interactions and acts to invisibly disarm and confuse normative explanations. These, I think, are Lefebvre's rhythms, and as he describes above – they are obscure, but they need not be a secret.

Throughout this book, by using a mobilities framework with a focus on *rhythms,* the invisible and unseen elements of these experiences can be articulated and revealed and can offer insights that deepen our knowledge of sexual harassment in transport environments. The focus of this chapter is to outline an in-depth mobilities perspective and the conceptual framework that will be used in subsequent chapters to make sense of women's experiences of sexual harassment on transport. This includes operationalising sociological understandings of mobilities, space, rhythms and temporalities. These conceptual dimensions are present throughout the book and inevitably overlap with one another; however, Chapter 4 ('before') focusses on women's experiences of navigating gendered urban *space*; Chapter 5 ('during') focusses on how experiences of sexual harassment on transport are shaped by *mobilities and rhythms*; Chapter 6 ('after') looks at how the impact of sexual harassment changes over *time*. As such, I will provide an overview of these concepts and how they will be operationalised in the corresponding order.

Space

As discussed in the previous chapter, sexual harassment has been theorised as a normalised part of everyday life for women in public spaces. Being a victim of sexual harassment can cause women to experience high levels of fear and vulnerability, leading them to undertake adaptive strategies that restrict their access to and enjoyment of public space (Boyer, 2022). Included in this 'safety-work' (Vera-Gray, 2018) is the preparation and planning involved before leaving the house (Kearl, 2010), and the regular assessment of surroundings for perceived risk. Common examples of this include choice of attire, avoiding certain areas, avoiding being alone (particularly after dark), using public transport instead of walking, or using private transport instead of public transport (Fileborn, 2016; Nicholls, 2017). Interestingly, those who did not undertake adaptive strategies, such as avoiding certain areas to avoid sexual harassment described making a conscious and active decision not to let the fear of male violence impede on their choices (Kearl, 2010). It was not that they had not considered it − it was that they had thought about it and, in an act of resistance, claimed their right to public space. Indeed, Koskela (2010) insists that fear should not be seen and portrayed as an essential female quality and the only experience women have when moving through public space. In her work 'Fear and its Others', she takes a social geographical approach and focusses on women's boldness and defiance in public space:

> Although it is probably true that all women feel fear sometimes in some situations, the feelings are rarely either/or. Even if part of the boldness is denial of fear *the feeling of boldness can still be real*. It could be taken seriously and respected as such. For some women, boldness can be seen as an absence of fear, an indicator of confidence, and not an attitude defined in terms of standing-up to fear. What if we try to look at this side of the story: How does it feel not to be afraid? How do we describe women laughing when they meet men down a dark alley? Can we speak about women saying it never occurred to them that they ought to be afraid? Can we talk about young women … who say that they own the city they live in? (Koskela, 2010, p. 305)

This book focusses on incidents of sexual harassment, and as such, many of the stories in the book are laced with fear – anxieties brought to the forefront by the subject matter. But bearing Koskela's question in mind helps illustrate what these intrusions are disrupting: women's boldness, a sense of freedom and ownership of the city. It also encourages us to avoid inadvertently naturalising female fear as the normal or only response and makes room for the complexity of women's gendered interactions in public space.

To explore these dynamics in public space, we must first conceptualise space as alive, eventful and in flux, rather than static and apolitical. In Lefebvre's (1991) work *The Production of Space*, he highlights the conceptual fragmentation that exists around the concept, calling for a reconciliation of physical space (nature), mental space (formal abstractions about space) and social space (the space of human interaction). Conceptualising space by combining these modalities allows for an intellectual approach that challenges dominant ideas of space as fixed. These notions tend to ignore how space itself is perceived and conceived, and how that can determine the interactions that occur within it. Similarly, feminist geographer Doreen Massey (1984, 2013) forwarded the idea that space is dynamic and important in the way in which we organise our lives and how society interacts. She argues that space is the dimension of multiplicity, presenting us with the question of the social and is not so much a physical locality as relations between human beings: the product of our relations with each other. I find these conceptualisations of space useful for underscoring the importance of the *social space* of the London Underground. It is, to use Lefebvre's (1991, p. 87) words, a space that constitutes 'great movements, vast rhythms, immense waves – these all collide and "interfere" with one another ...'. Knowing this, it is difficult to dispute the idea that it is generative and active in shaping the way sexual harassment is perpetrated and experienced in its milieu.

In the previous chapter, I described the London Underground as a semi-public space. Urban environments are composed of various spatial domains, often categorised as public, semi-public/semi-private and private places, varying from free to limited and exclusive access. Historically, public space has been observed as 'open space'. However, in the context of neoliberal urbanism (which sees the application of neoliberal economic principles applied to the urban environment), cities are becoming increasingly restructured around the proponents of privatisation, gentrification and commodification. As such, semi-public spaces that are managed privately or publicly-privately, are increasing (Nissen, 2008; Pratt, 2017). Despite its name, public transport sits within this categorisation. Both public and semi-public spaces can be considered the realms of unfocussed interactions between anonymous strangers (Goffman, 1971). In her book on street harassment, Brooks Gardner (1995, p. 44) describes these places as:

> [...] regions that are simultaneously everyone's and no one's, to which all are theoretically allowed access. Yet they are also sites for mockery and humiliation, the threat of interpersonal violence, verbal insults and injuries, avoidances and shunnings and the mere withholding of the rituals of civility.

This is significant, as despite many spaces being labelled as public and supposedly demonstrating freedom and access to all, they are often exclusionary to certain sectors of the population, whether due to discomfort, intimidation, or fear of real danger. Thereby these places remain public but are not freely utilised by everyone equally. Mitchell (1995) writes about how historically, women, men of ethnic minorities, and sexual dissidents have had to fight for access to the public sphere. This concept of public spaces as sites of struggle and exclusion is well-documented and often dominates urban politics, with particular focus on marginalised groups such as people who are homeless (Doherty et al., 2008), young people (Malone & Hasluck, 1998), sex workers (Hubbard, 2012), LGBTQ persons (Binnie & Skeggs, 2004; Hubbard, 2001), ethnic minorities (Peters, 2011), people with a lower income (Bancroft, 2002) and women (Massey, 1994; Wilson, 2001). Wilson (1991, p. 80) argues that whilst women have flourished in the city, they are still negotiating the contradictions of urban spaces and are not 'full citizens in the sense that they have never been granted full and free access to the streets'. Therefore, sexual harassment forms part of the wider (gender) politics of urban space. As a semi-public space, the Underground is theoretically accessible to anyone who can pay the travel fare. And yet, incidents of sexual harassment on the network implicate women's experiences of access to this space, making it fraught with negotiations of the right to be private in public. Whilst critiquing the physical nature of the space of the Underground is integral to understanding the (gendered) behaviours that occur within it, I contend that to understand sexual harassment in a peripatetic environment or 'on the move', a more appropriately nuanced conceptual framework is needed.

Mobilities: Rhythm and Friction

Drawing on a mobilities perspective to understand sexual harassment 'on the move' in a transit environment is highly fitting and yet this framework has scarcely been applied. Here, I will introduce a broader mobilities perspective, and then connect this with what it reveals about gendered access to the city. The mobilities paradigm or 'mobility turn' (Urry, 2000) in the social sciences sought to address the complex yet neglected role that mobilities, or the movement of people and things, play in the (re)configuration of social interactions and the social world. Bringing together social science and transport approaches, mobilities studies often connect the concepts of time and space, aiming to challenge the 'static' nature of social sciences, and the lack of social consideration of transport planners (Larsen et al., 2006). This approach drew attention to the significance of travel, automobility (Lumsden, 2015; Urry, 2004, 2006) and the practices of public transport in urban spaces (Bissell, 2018; Urry, 2007). It also asks us to attend to the affective and atmospheric experience of movement and transport (Cresswell, 2010). As an essential part of the urban fabric of any city, public transportation systems enable the movement of people and link activity in the rest of the city – connecting work, leisure and home. Yet despite this, Larsen et al. (2006, p. 3) argue that travel has (outside of mobilities studies) been seen as '… a neutral set of technologies and processes …' and that consequently the analysis of social interactions and encounters that occur when on the move has been largely neglected.

   In relation to urban mobilities, modernity caused a change in how people travelled, and therefore how they interacted whilst on the move, creating 'new mobilities' (Sheller & Urry, 2006) and sociabilities (Bissell, 2010). In a nutshell, modernisation accelerated the pace of life in the city. A key component of this was the Victorian railway, which mechanised mobility and formed a 'new connectedness' as masses of people were able to move more freely through extended time and space. As well as this evolved accessibility, rail travel created new sites of sociability where large numbers of strangers were impelled together in an enclosed space (Bissell, 2010; Urry, 2007), and bodies in carriages became 'anonymised parcels of flesh', passively avoiding each other (Thrift, 1996). The carriage moving rapidly through space was also a source of anxiety, forcing travellers to viscerally feel the fast-paced individuality of the city. The railway carriage acted to embody the urban experience of simultaneous confinement and exposure (Barrow, 2015).

During this period, limitation on mobility was a crucial means of the subordination and exclusion of women from the public realm. The introduction of rail travel had a substantial impact on women's mobility and access to public space as it shifted the boundaries of acceptability. Waiting for and being on transport provided a legitimate purpose to be in public space, and women were able to interact and engage with strangers, a privilege that was previously reserved for men. However, Victorian rail compartments were both public and highly intimate spaces and these new spatial and social dynamics, where men and women who were strangers found themselves in close proximity (Urry, 2007), led to intense cultural anxiety and moral panic around women's sexuality, vulnerability and the potential for sexual violence. This was particularly true for women travelling alone who were often regarded as inviting sexual attention (Barrow, 2015). It is important to consider that whilst the introduction of rail travel increased mobilities and provided a legitimate purpose for women to be in the public arena, the lack of safety associated with the space of the rail carriage and reports that emphasised the danger for female travellers, acted as a paternalistic form of social control, curtailing women's movements, and discouraging them from public space.

As well as the development of rail travel, over time there have been significant advancements in both gender relations and the nature of mobility. The development of the motorcar and automobility has had a significant impact on the design and everyday experience of cities (Gottdeiner & Hutchinson, 2006) and personal mobility. Graves-Brown (2000, p. 157) states that the car can be viewed as a 'mobile personal space' that is not to be challenged or invaded. As Lumsden (2009, p. 45) understands it, 'the private car is an instrument for exercising our right to unrestricted individual motion'. Unequal access to automobility has been considered, most commonly in relation to social class (Gartman, 2004), and work that has explored the relationship between gender and automobility has focussed on the increased mobility and freedom from the domestic sphere that the car has provided for women (Wosk, 2001). Yet others have argued that women have historically had limited access to automobility, with car ownership being perceived as a masculine venture, with male journeying to work prioritised over women's journeys to service the domestic requirements of a household (Lumsden, 2009). This has meant that both historically and in the present day, on a global scale, women are more dependent on public transport than men (Dobbs, 2005; Levin, 2019).

The dialogue around women in public and liminal arenas such as transport has also evolved significantly over time. It has become less preoccupied with identifying areas of exclusion and more attention has been given to how women negotiate and navigate these spaces. Rather than being confined to the domestic sphere, women's increased journeying and nomadic tendencies have developed (Tilley & Houston, 2016), and access and relative safety have improved over time. Yet the persistence and prevalence of sexually harassing behaviour within transport spaces demonstrates that it is still structured in a way (spatially and socially) that is conducive to these behaviours being perpetrated. I contend that these intersections of space and mobilities and their role in shaping gendered experiences can be explored more comprehensively by using the concept of *rhythms*.

Earlier, I mentioned Henri Lefebvre's *Production of Space*. His work on rhythms or *Rhythmanalysis* (Lefebvre, 2004), is lesser known, and yet 'This little book does not conceal its ambition. It proposes nothing less than to found a science, a new field of knowledge [*savoir*]: the analysis of rhythms; with practical consequences' (p. 3). Simply written, Rhythmanalysis 'deepens the study of everyday life' (Lefebvre, 2004, p. 73). The concept of rhythms will be applied throughout this book to explore various aspects of sexual harassment on the Underground, including how women experience and move through urban space; how the rhythms of the city and the Underground mean sexual harassment is perpetrated and experienced in particular ways at particular times, and how rhythms and temporalities intersect in the remembering of sexual harassment. Lefebvre (2004) states that 'Everywhere where there is interaction between a place, a time and an expenditure of energy, there is rhythm' (p. 15), and this is nowhere more explicit than in a bustling urban space, especially a transport system like the Underground. These rhythms are present in a multiplicity of forms; they can be biological, psychological, social and mechanical; corporeal, natural, institutional and collective, differing in characteristics such as frequency, intensity and regularity. They can be intermittent, volatile and surging and they continuously interact, harmonise and clash with one another (Edensor, 2010). These collections of rhythms '... form the polyrhythmic ensembles from which spatiotemporal consistencies and places emerge' (Schwanen et al., 2012, p. 2066), essentially constituting the ambiance and feel of a place, which in turn impacts the social dynamics and interactions that occur within it. As Highmore (2002) considers, rhythm analysis has the ability to reveal the *politics of pace*.

Lefebvre's (1991) interest in rhythms is already apparent in his previous work as he describes spaces as: 'great movements, vast rhythms, immense waves – these all collide and 'interfere' with one another ...' (p. 87). In *Elements of Rhythmanalysis*, he expands on the notion of space as dynamic. Indeed, rhythms fundamentally challenge the notion that space is fixed and demonstrate that the urban field is in motion, rather than a mute staging. It is both transforming and transformative. This brings us to Lefebvre's insistence that first and foremost rhythmanalysis demands that time and space be regarded as interrelated in order to not only deal with the spatial, but also the temporal order of everyday life. As Mulicek et al. (2015, p. 116) elaborate 'the city can be defined not only through its spatial attributes but also through its affiliation to a particular spatiotemporal system'. This linking of time and space removes the idea of self-contained moments and establishes that rhythms cannot be detached from one another and should be observed and listened to 'within wholes' (Lefebvre, 2004, p. 24). This holds relevance when observing how the activity of the city above impacts the rhythms of the Underground network. For example, during the Monday to Friday 'working week', the flow and temporality of capital takes priority, and business hours create 'rush hours' on the Tube network, that possess an entirely different ambiance and normative mode of behaviour in comparison to the 'night tube' on weekends, where sociabilities and rhythms are largely impacted by the night-time economy. These spatial, mobile and temporal dimensions intersect and impress on how sexual harassment is perpetrated and experienced. In the same vein, when considering the dominant rhythms that regulate everyday city life, urban public transport schedules are an example of institutionally inscribed urban cyclical time (Mulicek et al., 2015; Schwanen et al., 2012). The rhythms of the London Underground are dominated by attributes of rationalisation, punctuality and calculability, which Simmel (1997, p. 177) recognised as necessary to avoid 'inextricable chaos' (you only have to envision London on the day of Tube strikes or delays to know this holds true). These regular and repetitive rhythms of the Underground allow a sense of predictability that is highly valued by commuters and creates a sense of certainty or everyday 'ontological predictability and security' (Edensor, 2010, p. 8). Yet this rationalism and functionalism exist in constant tension with the corporeal rhythms of the autonomous individuals that move through the system, with an ever-present risk of disjuncture.

Lefebvre puts great emphasis on corporeality, claiming that capturing, expressing and understanding urban rhythms is always done through the body. He states that 'at no moment have the analysis of rhythms and the rhythmanalysis project lost sight of the body' (Lefebvre, 2004, p. 67). He emphasises the necessity to always locate the body as a first point of reference and 'the tool for subsequent investigations' (Lefebvre, 2004, p. 12). As Prior (2011, p. 205) considers, rhythmanalysis: '… locates the body as a constant reference point for the alliances and conflicts of rhythms – not just the anatomical, physiological body, but the body as being-in-the-world, perceiving, acting, thinking and feeling'. Essentially, Lefebvre (2004) suggests that the 'rhythmanalyst' uses their body as a 'metronome' (p. 19), a continuous position through which rhythms are known and expressed. With regard to *polyrhythmia*, that is, multiple rhythms, it is significant to consider biological rhythms and how they interact with broader or external social rhythms: or, how biological rhythms are impacted by the social environment and vice-versa. Because rhythms are multitudinous and coexist, they can be aligned, or they can be in discord. Lefebvre suggests that the body can be used to recognise both when rhythms are operating in their natural state or in harmony (eurythmia) and when there is a disruption and breaking apart of rhythms (arrhythmia). The second is perhaps an easier task, as he considers: 'we are only conscious of most of our rhythms when we begin to suffer from some irregularity' (Lefebvre, 2004, p. 77). A recognition of the role of bodily rhythms and their interaction with external rhythms is significant in advancing debates on the negotiation and impact of sexual harassment. For example, when looking at the immediate impact of sexual harassment, rhythms reveal how women's actions (e.g. 'freezing') are not simply a 'natural' corporeal response out of fear but are also implicated by uncertainty as to what is happening to them and the anticipation of other peoples' behaviour within a particular space. This is exactly what I experienced when the man masturbated at me on the bus (described in the opening vignettes). Lefebvre's acknowledgement of the coexistence of biological and social rhythms demonstrates the embodied relationship between individuals and the spatiotemporal nature of the city.

The body is the point of contact for these rhythms and often the site of collision and arrhythmia, as demonstrated by the women's stories presented in this book.

Since the 'mobilities turn', a significant body of work has focussed on or recognised the importance of *immobilities*, or how mobilities can be limited and disrupted (Adey, 2006; Hannam et al., 2006). Hubbard and Lilley (2004) proffer that where there is speed, there also exists interruptions and slowness, and Sheller and Urry (2006) consider how feminist work has been significant in drawing attention to inequalities in mobility (Ahmed, 2004; Morley, 2000). As Skeggs (2004, p. 49) states: 'Mobility and control over mobility both reflect and reinforce power. Mobility is a resource to which not everyone has an equal relationship'. Therefore, a lack of, or disruption to mobility and access can act to reinforce social exclusion. As the stories presented in this book show, sexual harassment often forced women to slow down or restrict their mobilities, therefore this is an important notion to consider further.

A concept drawn from mobilities studies that is useful to conceptualise immobility, or a slowing down of mobility, is Cresswell's (2010) notion of *friction*. In his work on the politics of mobility, Cresswell deconstructs mobility into six parts: motive force, velocity, rhythm, route, experience and friction. Here, rhythm and friction are both recognised as important components. Friction is described as a social and cultural phenomenon that can be lived and felt when our mobility is prevented or slowed down, both involuntarily and out of choice. He offers examples of encountering suspicion at border control or stopping to take in a scenic view. Mobilising the concept of friction with regard to sexual harassment on the Underground, this notion of slowing down holds relevance, as women's mobilities are often interrupted or disrupted, rather than stopped altogether, leading to 'blockages' or 'coagulations' (Adey, 2006; Marston et al., 2005) in mobility, which can cause anxiety and frustration. Cresswell (2014) also discusses how those with power can slow down or restrict the mobility of others by increasing friction. This is significant to the discussion in Chapter 4 of women's freedom and ability to engage freely in the city without the risk of male intrusion, as (fear of) sexual harassment is often experienced as a friction and interference with both women's ideas of and actual freedom and movement in the city. Friction is also used throughout Chapter 5 to demonstrate how experiencing sexual harassment can cause a slowing down of women's urban mobilities. The concept of *friction* illustrates how, as discussed above, women's mobilities often remain punctuated with fear and disruption. However, these notions of mobility are not complete without a consideration of the temporal dynamics at play.

Temporalities

In this book, temporalities are significant in our lens of analysis to expand knowledge of the occurrences of sexual harassment on transport. I want to first draw attention to how the temporalities of the Underground reflect the disciplinary pacing of the city above. In the modern capitalist city, time is money. The Underground serves the city its workers, like veins to the heart, and thus, unwavering efficiency and predictability are paramount for maximum productivity.

It also incites the notion of time spent travelling (or time not at the destination) as 'dead time' and something to be minimised. In a highly affective atmosphere, these temporal policies become embodied by commuters. As we see in some of the women's stories in later chapters, many regular Tube travellers plan their journey's down to the minute, leaving little time for disruption of any kind. In the space of the carriage, agitated bodies are forced into corporeal immobility, and, in this physical-psycho-spatial nexus, many commuters actively disassociate in order to subjectively speed up their journey. Consequently, there is significant disdain towards anything that disrupts this collective condition – something that many of the women we hear from in this book were acutely aware of. Time, when considered in this way, significantly implicates the response of both victims and bystanders of sexual harassment on the Tube. Thus, I argue later, that this disciplining, standardising temporality breeds inertia and apathy in the face of sexual harassment happening 'on the move' and we see an interesting manifestation of 'moral minimalism', where the preferred reaction to wrongdoing is the least extreme, and people are reluctant to exercise social control against one another (Baumgartner, 1988). Baumgartner's work on moral minimalism centres around understanding suburban order, however, it is startlingly applicable to the temporally implicated social order of the Tube. She states: 'The order ... does not arise from intimacy and connectedness, but rather from some of the very things more often presumed to bring about conflict and violence – transiency, fragmentation, isolation, atomization, and indifference among people' (p. 134).

As well as this underlying (or overarching) temporality, we can observe various ways in which time structures experiences of sexual harassment. Firstly, the circadian temporalities of the city rhythms impact on how sexual harassment manifests differently at particular times of day. Secondly, the Underground is a transitory, mobile place with a temporal nature seemingly dominated by speed, which shapes how women negotiate harassment. Thirdly, women's subjective experiences of time are impacted when they are exposed to sexual harassment. Finally, as time structures human experience, I use it as a concept in the form of memory in order to analyse the impact of sexual harassment when looking back and looking forward.

The role of spatial-temporalities (or time–space geography) has, to an extent, also been considered as a significant factor that impacts women's experiences of (fear of) crime in transit, with substantial attention paid to understanding both environmental factors that increase levels of fear and perceived risk (poor lighting, lack of visibility, etc.) (Gilchrist et al., 1998; Loukaitou-Sideris, 1999; Pain, 1997; Valentine, 1990), and when actual incidents of crime in transit environments occur (Ceccato, 2017). Studies have often focussed on the impact of the spatial and temporal attributes of criminal activity, as discussed earlier in regard to routine activity theory (Ceccato & Uittenbogaard, 2014; Cohen & Felson, 1979; Felson et al., 1994). In this piece of work, it is rhythms that intimately connect space and time, recognising that sexual harassment happens in a particular space, in a particular way at certain times of day. During morning and evening rush hours the Underground takes on what Bissell (2010) describes as characteristic of commuter train travel, where bodies are densely packed in and pressed up against one another in a confined space. This proximity (alongside the sociabilities it induces) permits sexual harassment to be perpetrated in a particularly physical way, commonly in the form of groping, frotteuring and grabbing. In the evening, especially at weekends, the carriages take on an altered, more affable and sociable atmosphere, and sexual harassment often comes in the form of alcohol-fuelled interactions, more overt and often verbal. In the middle of the day and late at night carriages are often relatively quiet, to the point where it is not unusual to be alone or with only one other person in the carriage. It is in this spatiotemporal setting that exposure or masturbation is more commonly perpetrated. This highlights how it is necessary to consider not only space but also temporalities in order to understand the nature of sexual harassment on the London Underground.

As well as occurring in specific ways at particular times, sexual harassment on the Underground is happening within a space of abundant and seemingly high-speed mobility (Auge, 1995; Urry, 2007). It is fast and repetitive, a system through which an individual can (generally) move with speed and predictability. In such an environment, Urry (2007, p. 98) states 'Time becomes a resource … consumed, deployed, exhausted', or rather, time becomes a resource to be measured and managed. The mechanised movement of rail travel saw a rise in the value of *speed* of travel (Thrift, 1996; Virilio, 1986), with the presumption that time spent travelling is 'dead time' (Urry, 2007, p. 99) and should therefore be reduced. Whilst this has been challenged, and the pleasures of time spent travelling highlighted (Lyons & Urry, 2005), on the London Underground, the normative temporal order (re)produces the notion that the less time spent travelling, the better. This in turn impacts the sociabilities that occur within the space, with Goffman's (1963) concept of 'civil inattention' (a deference owed to strangers in public space) and Simmel's (1903) 'metropolitan individuality' dominating the social scenes in carriages, allowing passengers a predictable journey with minimal unnecessary interaction or interruption. This is significant in three ways. Firstly, as we will see in Chapters 5 and 6, some women did not challenge harassers or immediately report to authorities due to not wanting to prolong their journey and further disrupt their mobilities. Furthermore, some were unwilling to speak out when experiencing sexual harassment, for fear of disrupting the decorum of the carriage. Here, the temporal nature of the Tube has a strong impact on the sociabilities that occur within it, and consequently shapes how women react to sexual harassment. Finally, some women felt they did not have time to react before the perpetrator slipped away with the crowd.

Rail travel is said to have changed notions of the relationship between time and space (Thrift, 1996). Urry (2007) recognises the sensory perception of the speed of travel, and Watts (2006) discusses how the experience and passing of train time have interesting characteristics, including the stretching out and compressing of journey times. In Chapter 5, I show how some women, whilst experiencing sexual harassment, felt like time had slowed down, or their regular and routine journeys were prolonged. In some ways, this links back to the concept of friction, yet it takes a more abstract and perceptual form in the sense that the journey itself is not being prolonged, but rather the subjective experience of the temporal is causing time to slacken and drag.

Another way in which temporalities are key to this research is that they allow us to explore how the *impact* of sexual harassment alters and is (re)negotiated across time. This is explored in Chapter 6 through the social concept of *memory*. The concept of memory relates to the way in which we reconceptualise the past, present and future. The temporal aspect of memory relates to how and what is remembered over time and the impact that has (Adam, 1991). It helps to conceptualise how incidents of sexual harassment are remembered and negotiated over time and how they impact on women's experiences of urban space. It also highlights how experiences of sexual violence are often re-defined as such after a prolonged period of time, based both on personal life trajectories and societal context (an example of this is how, in the wake of the #MeToo movement, many women began recognising historical workplace experiences as sexual harassment). Chapter 6 explores how the memory of an event of sexual harassment impacts on women's future behaviour within the space of the Underground. It aims to understand the negotiations that women undertake in order to 'deal with' the incidents of sexual harassment and claim back their mobility and freedom, and how this often changes over time and space. It permits a move beyond discussing women's access, fear and vulnerability and allows an examination of how sexual harassment in public space is negotiated and resisted, and how the experiences or memories are also suppressed and thus embolden women. I use the conceptual framework structured around space and mobilities to offer a unique temporal analysis of the impact of sexual harassment.

Each of the concepts outlined here play a role in how sexual harassment is shaped and experienced on the Underground. To summarise: *Space* is conceptualised to be active in (re)producing gender inequalities, in this case, affecting the manifestation of sexual harassment; *mobilities* and *rhythms* are active across space and show how women's experiences of sexual harassment are shaped by and impact on their movements through this space; *temporalities* allow insight into how, over time, women negotiate the impact and memory of sexual harassment as they move through the city and the Underground. This conceptual framework opens up a new angle from which to understand incidences of sexual harassment on the Tube network, by locating them within the rhythmic, spatiotemporal environment. As we journey through women's negotiations of urban space and incidents of sexual harassment on public transport, this framework assists in drawing out the nuanced and often 'invisible' or overlooked elements of these experiences.

Chapter 4

'Before': Gendered Experiences of Urban Space

Abstract

This chapter draws on empirical data from women's stories as we start on the 'journey' of experiences of sexual harassment. This chapter focusses on the 'before', as I present women's accounts of everyday life *moving* around London and participating in the rhythmic ensemble of the city. It demonstrates how the city remains a gendered environment that induces both fear and freedom and contextualises the (physical and mental) landscape in which incidents of sexual harassment occur. I will draw on theoretical approaches relating to the emergence of urban modernity in order to contextualise how the social, spatial and temporal conditions in the historical metropolis led to the advent of new sociabilities and modes of being in public life that still influence interactions today. Acknowledging that this remains gendered, I call on the literary character of the *flâneur* to critically analyse women's past and present mobilities in the city. I simultaneously incorporate Lefebvre's concept of rhythm to illustrate how the anticipation and expectation of sexual harassment impact women's mobilities so intimately that it constitutes their normative urban rhythms. By exploring women's wider lives in the context of movement and mobilities in the city, this chapter demonstrates the gendered nature of everyday life in the urban environment, including how the anticipation and perceived risk of sexual harassment are experienced and negotiated as an omnipresent possibility.

Keywords: Sexual harassment; flâneur; flâneuse; urban space; rhythmanalysis

Mind the Gender Gap: A Mobilities Perspective of Sexual Harassment on the
London Underground, 51–74
doi:10.1108/978-1-83753-026-720241004

I'm fairly fearless when I travel around London because I know its rhythms. And it really does have its own rhythms. (Laya)

[…] in London I stride with purpose and ownership wherever I go, I take no prisoners, these are my streets. (Kath)

The first three chapters have laid the contextual and theoretical foundations on which to present women's experiences of sexual harassment on the London Underground. Throughout, I have argued that it is necessary to locate these incidents in women's broader, everyday orbit and daily urban mobilities. The aim of this chapter is to understand how women experience and negotiate London and the Underground in everyday life. I start this chapter by introducing the concept of the flâneur, a 19th century Parisian character associated with the modern city. Whilst the flâneur originated in a specific historical and cultural context, it is a relevant concept to discern the modern urban experience and the way in which individuals interact with and perceive the city. It acts as a useful conceptual lens through which to understand women's experiences in London *and* on the Tube in the present day. We will look at their negotiations of London 'above ground', tuning into the rhythms that are implicit in moulding these urban experiences. Then, we will focus more specifically on women's perceptions and use of the Underground, and how it can be experienced as a site of boredom, anxiety and pleasure. The chapter concludes by showing how women's anticipation of gendered violence in public space acts to both constitute and disrupt their rhythms and limit their freedom in the city and impinges on the optimistic possibility of a modern day 'flâneuse'. Filtering everyday lives and movements around the city through this conceptual framework allows an understanding of women's everyday gendered mobilities in urban space. This chapter is the start of the journey: the 'before' and the prelude, acting to set the urban scene within which incidents of sexual harassment on the Tube are perpetrated and experienced.

The Flâneur

the female flâneur's desire for her own exploration of the world ends where it encounters its limits in male pedestrians and fantasies, assaulting, annoying, disturbing and perpetually evaluating her in the street. Gleber (1998, p. 8)

Coined in the 19th century, a period of mass urbanisation, the concept or literary device of the flâneur remains a key figure in literature on modernity and urbanisation (Wilson, 1991). The first thorough description of the flâneur comes from Baudelaire (1964) in his essay 'The Painter of Modern Life'. He draws his inspiration from Edgar Allen Poe's (1840) short story, *The Man of the Crowd*, where the crowd is symbolic of the modern city, and the protagonist acts as a new urban type: the unattached observer or stroller. Used to portray a Parisian character in the city, Baudelaire (1964, p. 9) describes him as 'the passionate spectator ... to see the world, to be at the centre of the world, and yet to remain hidden from the world ...'. This draws attention to two key qualities that constitute the act of *flânerie*: walking and looking yet remaining detached – characteristics that became possible with the emergence of modernity. Walter Benjamin (1982) further explores the flâneur in relation to modernism in *The Arcades Project*, using it as a point from which to investigate the impact of urban life on the human psyche. The rise of the modern city became equated with public life and the creation of conditions of co-presence (Crang, 2001), leading to the emergence of new sociabilities epitomised by Goffman's (1963) concept of 'civil inattention'. Of all the literature regarding social interaction and modernity, Georg Simmel's (1903) essay *The Metropolis and Mental Life* is perhaps most poignant. He declares that the new urban condition of 'metropolitan individuality' and the 'blasé attitude' urbanites possess are established by the existence of increased tempo and exposure to constant external stimuli (Simmel, 1903). This is a socio-spatial nexus in which the flâneur thrives. With his contentment in the crowd and affinity for transient interactions, the flâneur is often proclaimed as the 'modern hero' (Urry, 2007, p. 69). However, perhaps unsurprisingly, the experience of the flâneur was recognised as distinctly male. As Wolff (1985, p. 40) considers: 'these heroes of modernity ... share the possibility and the prospect of lone travel, of voluntary uprooting, of anonymous arrival at a new place. They are of course, all men'.

The Elusive Flâneuse?

The flâneur continues to be used as a tool to examine a variety of social concerns in urban spaces. In his article 'Disabling the Flâneur', Serlin (2006) situates the flâneur as occupying able-bodied privilege and calls for the inclusion of sensorial and tactile experiences of disabled people in narratives of urban modernity. Within the vein of sensorial understandings of the city, Boutin (2012, p. 124) asks the question whether the 'lure of the visual has blinded us to other significant aspects of urban experience' and asks that we focus on the non-visual, sensorial ways in which the flâneur experiences the city. There is also a faction of work that argues how flânerie can act as an alternative way to collect qualitative data in urban space (Beck & Sznaider, 2006; Jenks & Neves, 2000; Rizk & Birioukov, 2017). These works follow the lead of Walter Benjamin's own assertion that the action of flânerie includes observation, listening, reading (of the city and texts) and producing texts (Frisby, 1994). Surprisingly, in the realm of criminology, there has been relatively little uptake of the flâneur as a conceptual tool. An exception comes from Lynes et al. (2019) who, in conjunction with an ultra-realist perspective, explore how serial killers operate in the modern urban landscape. There is, however, a significant body of work elsewhere that has explored the gendered nature of the flâneur and flânerie. I hope that by connecting the flâneur with the negotiation and experiences of sexual harassment in the city, it demonstrates the scope of the concept in criminological inquiry.

Encapsulating the liberating, sensuous enjoyment that can be found from walking aimlessly and anonymously through the urban spectacle, feminist critiques argue that this act of 'flânerie' is a manifestation of male privilege and leisure (Elkin, 2016; Wolff, 1985) and that the ability to be private in public is not equally enjoyed by women. In her essay 'The Invisible Flâneuse?', Janet Wolff (1985) employs the concept of the 'flâneuse' to symbolise women's restricted participation in public space as well as to highlight the gender bias in classical literature on modern cities. To put it simply, women did not have access to public space in the same way that men did, and their experiences were often marginalised and overlooked. Gendered divisions between men and women in the 19th century were pervasive, and the 'separate spheres model' (Bookman & Morgen, 1987) – the binary division between public and private spaces – is crucial to understanding how women have been confined to the domestic sphere whilst men have been public figures in public space. Because of this exclusion, when women did enter the streets, it was often under the endurance of the male gaze (Hubbard, 2012). As Pollock (1988, p. 259) suggests 'the gaze of the flâneur articulates and produces a masculine sexuality, which in the modern sexual economy enjoys the freedom to look, appraise and possess ...'. Unlike the male flâneur, for women in the 19th century, visibility on the streets was commonly equated with moral laxity and sexual accessibility (Brooks Gardner, 1995; Solnit, 2001). By being in the city alone (particularly at night), women ran risks to their safety, reputation and virtue. Due to the voyeuristic nature of the city and the divisive gender relations of the time, it was almost impossible for women to stroll unnoticed through the streets (Wolff, 1985).

Over the past few decades, arguments have emerged contending that there is, and always has been, a female flâneur: the *flâneuse*. In her book *The Sphinx in the City*, British sociologist Elizabeth Wilson (1991) considers the possibility of the flâneuse on the grounds that whilst the public domain was perceived as male-dominated and potentially dangerous for women, in comparison to suburban and rural domesticity, it provided opportunity and freedom, an escape from restrictive, often exploitative familial and patriarchal relations. With the city providing an escape from the spatial confines of home, women gradually became more visible participants in the urban scene, in part due to modern consumption transpiring as a female leisure activity (in particular department stores and cinemas). This meant that women were permitted to enter the city whilst retaining their respectability (Chaney, 1983; Felski, 1995). Yet with regard to flânerie, this was a freedom afforded within the confines of consumerism. Therefore, whilst recognising the growth of a female presence in the city, it did not allow women the fleeting, anonymous encounters or purposeless strolling that men were accustomed to (Solnit, 2001; Wolff, 1985).

In her book *Flâneuse: Women Walk the City in Paris, New York, Tokyo, Venice and London*, Lauren Elkin (2016) traces how various women throughout history have engaged with the city. An excellent illustration is that of the modernist writer Virgina Woolf, who drew immense vitality, pleasure and inspiration from her walking in London. Woolf's (2006) musings on London are most vividly portrayed in the collection of essays entitled *The London Scene*. In her work, Woolf describes the anonymity of London in the 1930s as a desirable aspect of the city, allowing her to be freed from the subjugation of her own identity. Similar sentiments weave through the women's narratives presented below. Elkin also offers the example of the French novelist George Sand who famously dressed up as a man in order to roam the streets in 19th century Paris. Whilst Elkin uses Sand as an example of how women negotiated and transgressed boundaries and gender constraints, Wolff's (1985) position would argue that this once again proves how women could not stroll alone in the city, pertaining to the idea that the flâneuse was non-existent. Yet Elkin (2016, p. 11) considers that 'perhaps the answer is not to attempt to make a woman fit a masculine concept, but to redefine the concept itself'. The concepts of the flâneur and the flâneuse are useful tools of analysis that can be employed to explore gender relations in public urban space and women's right to the city. With their fluidity and continual reworking, the concepts will be engaged alongside rhythms when analysing the accounts of contemporary London presented in the following sections of this chapter. By showing how women experience and move through the city and the Underground on a day-to-day basis, I aim to actively redefine how we think about women in public urban space by recognising the freedom and pleasures that coexist and intertwine with the potential dangers of urban life.

Gendered Mobilities in the City: London Life – Arriving, Thriving, Surviving

> *I think if you're trying to capture the vibe of London you have to more understand why people come here to begin with. And I think that's a mixture. I think London has this glamorised thing of lights, big city, prospects of jobs and money and excitement. And at the same time, all those big lights and the hustle and bustle makes it easier for people to come to the city to disappear … whether that's good or bad.* (Ally)

This chapter now moves on to expose the strain between pleasure and anxiety that many women negotiate in 21st century London. Life here is varied, turbulent and fragmentary. Yet, viewing these experiences through the lens of rhythmanalysis and flânerie we can begin to discern patterns that help understand women's mobilities in urban space. We will start broadly at the epidermis of the city, traversing through both the imaginings and footsteps on the streets of London, exploring how the rhythms of the city are felt and negotiated and are implicit in the formation of particular experiences of the city. We will then delve deeper to explore women's understandings of and interactions with the London Underground and weave through positions of stress, anxiety, comfort and pleasure. We see that the Tube is something to be both endured and enjoyed. As we near the end of the chapter, I will hone the focus towards how freedom is often negotiated amidst a peripheral or lingering sense of fear, and how the anticipation of gendered violence acts to constitute, disrupt and shift women's urban rhythms.

As discussed, the flâneur is inextricably linked with modernity, a period of mass movement from traditional rural living to the city (Baudelaire, 1864; Giddens, 1990; Simmel, 1903). This appeal of the urban continues today.

Embodying the compelling magnetism of a global metropolis, for many, London whistled promise, and for a number of women, the prospect of life in the city was spoken of as a childhood dream, an exciting next step. Arriving and surviving in the city was symbolic of progression and independence.

> Rachel, a 31-year-old academic who grew up in a small town in Essex described how she felt before moving to London 10 years ago: 'It's such a childhood dream to be here and it represents a lot in that way of getting out of the small town. London always seemed like the place to be and I felt like my life was about to begin, all these new opportunities ... I was ready to be in the big city'.

> Grace, 36, also grew up on the outskirts of the city and spoke about how as soon as she and her friends finished college they committed to their intentions to move to London: 'This strange little place where I'm from, everyone grows up and wants to come to London ... I was always drawn to London, there are so many opportunities here, I understand the pull'.

> Similarly, Cris, 28, now working as a nurse, said that after university 'it seemed like a really obvious choice to come to London, not too far away, a big city, lots of hospitals, job opportunities and I followed the crowd, a lot of people were coming to London'.

These imaginings of London mirror the emancipatory appeal of urbanity that began to transpire when the modern city came into being in the mid-19th century. A trace of this mentality lingers today, with the city representing financial and social opportunity, unmatched by rural or suburban places. For Rachel, Grace and Cris their perceptions of London and the anticipation of the possibilities it offered preceded its actuality and swayed them to pursue life in the big city. For others, circumstance rather than appeal brought them to London. This was the case for both Sheila and Alison who, being from the North of England, possessed a different perception of the city, holding a certain 'anti-urbanism' perspective (Thompson, 2009) with regard to London.

> Alison graduated university three years ago, aged 20 and accepted the first job offer she received, in London: 'London never appealed to me. I'd never wanted to live in London ... I struggled but, I gradually got more comfortable and now it feels like home, I love it, there's always something different, that's what I love'.

> Going through a hard time at home, Sheila, now 36, spontaneously took a summer job with a charity, expecting to hate it and only stay the season: 'I think I had this image in my head of London as being big horrible crazy smelly polluted and unfriendly. But I came to London that summer and I fell in love with the

place … I think it's opened my eyes to a very diverse, very vibrant culture and in fact there's always something to do, you're never bored and I've met really great people. I think moving here opened up a whole new world for me and it made me realise that there's a lot more to life'.

This relates closely to Simmel's (1903) theorisation that the urban initially induces shock and fear yet is often learnt to be appreciated. Indeed, an agglomeration of the opportunities and encapsulating urban buzz motivated these women to construct their space within the cityscape. Far from being exceptions, the allure of London as a city of prospects is far-reaching and attracts individuals from all over the world, which contributes significantly to its diversity and multiculturalism. These aspects were highlighted as defining factors contributing to the character of the city and are elements that many were proud of.

Kreeda, 25, working in student welfare who has grown up in London with Indian parents similarly said, 'It's so diverse. I'm not saying there isn't racism and homophobia, but I feel for the most part it's a very accepting city'.

When I asked Annie, 26, what kept drawing her back to London she said, 'I think it's the multiculturalism of London, that's what I really like is the mix of people, you don't get that elsewhere'.

Eliza, who has grown up in North London said, 'I love the multicultural-ness of it, the feeling of importance, almost like it's the centre of the universe, I like feeling like I'm at the centre of something'.

Sammi, 37, who grew up in London and is of British and Indian descent described what she liked about the city: 'its cultural diversity and acceptance … my experience of leaving London was always accompanied by a sharp rise in cultural ignorance, nationalism and whiteness. I would suddenly be complimented for being exotic'.

This 'commonplace diversity' (Wessendorf, 2014), contributes significantly to the alluring anonymity that London offers, ensuring a certain degree of ephemeral freedom when roaming the city.

As Dora, 30, mused: 'In London, everyone and no one fits in. Everyone and no one stands out'.

It is within this urban context that, despite the historical elusiveness of the flâneuse, we can catch glimpses of her in contemporary London.

Kath, 40, who grew up in London and recently moved away, said:
'What do I miss about London? I miss my freedom ... it's that
anonymity first of all, that makes you feel a bit freer. It's partly
the size and sheer volume of people and the extent of transience'.

One of the flâneur's most noteworthy characteristics is that they remain anonymous and detached whilst observing and strolling through the urban spectacle.
A number of women described how this was one of their favourite features of life
in London, with some specifically highlighting the pleasure in doing this alone,
as a solo venture.

Alison, from Huddersfield, said she would not have previously considered this appealing, but this changed since moving to London:
'I do stuff on my own now. I didn't used to like my own company
but now I walk around, explore, go to a few exhibitions by myself,
that's what I love ... I used to get really lost, but it was fun!'.

Becky, 31, considered how this sort of pursuit was particular to
urban space: 'Cities are good places to be if you like the outdoors.
In London you can walk everywhere if you're central. I try to walk
everywhere and take different routes. I like to be outdoors and
walking'.

When I asked Grace to describe what she liked about living in
London she answered: 'It's like the whole world has opened up.
Where can I go, what can I do? And that's what I love about London. You wander around and you don't know what you're going to
see around the corner, who you're going to bump into. I sometimes
think, I haven't had time just to walk around for a while, so I go
around and walk the streets and see what's going on'.

Made possible by significant progress in gender relations, women undoubtedly
have access to traverse and enjoy the public spaces of London. These experiences and the ability to walk unnoticed are in part permitted by one of the core
attributes of urban life: anonymity. As previously mentioned, this is also one of
the most salient characteristics of the flâneur (Baudelaire, 1964; Wilson, 1991).
Living in the city was defined by participants as permitting a certain amount of
privacy and freedom.

Demi, 38, describes how it 'gives people the space to be able to be
who they are, or who they want to be'.

Dora came to London from France 11 years ago when she was
19 and recalls how she felt liberated by walking through the streets,
particularly in comparison to other cities she'd lived in: 'The first
thing I noticed when I moved to London ... well I like to wear

small dresses and when I first moved here I noticed I wasn't getting harassed for wearing short skirts. I didn't get harassed on the streets, nobody gave a shit. The amount of shits people did not give was amazing'.

Becky, born in London and moving back to the city aged 23, reiterated this saying 'I feel a certain amount of freedom in the anonymity; nobody gives a shit about what you're doing ... nobody cares'.

This links again to Simmel's (1903) 'metropolitan individuality' and 'blasé outlook': the notion that modern urbanites treat those around them with ambivalence and indifference due to a filtering out of excess external stimuli.

Laya, 40, who moved to London 17 years ago considers this almost directly, as she stated: 'I don't think that people in London are particularly unfriendly, it's just the rush of the city and the stresses of living here that make people retreat into themselves ... that shield, it's a necessity, a resilience or protection thing'.

It became clear that Londoners themselves recognise that this attitude is often perceived as rude and unwelcoming by those unaccustomed to the fast and indifferent pace of the city.

Eliza considered this saying: 'There's this theory about how Londoners are really unfriendly, which in my experience just isn't true. I think actually Londoners are some of the friendliest, most welcoming people when you break that barrier'.

Sammi recognised how the collective enactment of these sociabilities creates certain expectations: 'I think this anonymity might have something to do with the fact that we're quite rude, for want of a better word. I think a lot of people who come from elsewhere say Londoners keep to themselves, mind their own business ... but it's quite normal and I do enjoy it. No one bothers you, it's a social norm you get used to, and I quite like it! You can go about your business and expect not to be interrupted'.

There is a clear correlation here with Goffman's (1963) theory of 'civil inattention'. Those who have become accustomed to this mode of being are able to appreciate that, whilst this type of sociability may seem averse and hostile, it is a highly functional, yet subtle, manner of communication (Bissell, 2010). This favourable notion towards sociabilities such as a 'blasé outlook' and 'civil inattention' offers a mode of being in the city that resonates with the comfort that the flâneur found in being anonymous in the crowd. The women describe their enjoyment at how being in a diverse metropolis affords them the privilege and pleasure of anonymity. This imitates Baudelaire's (1964, p. 9) depiction of the flâneur who likes 'to be at the centre of the world, and yet to remain hidden from the world ...'. As well as this pervasive anonymity, there were substantial references to the fleeting social intimacies that occur in everyday urban life, due to living in a state of almost constant co-presence (Crang, 2001).

> Eliza reflected on this: 'I think the lovely thing about London is that actually we're probably more used to people being in our personal space. I don't think twice if I'm squashed into a space and people are touching my arms and stuff ... I think most people in London will have an experience of a stranger being in their personal space, not on purpose but out of necessity. So, I think we're more tolerant of it than people in other places, which I think has its strengths and weaknesses, but I think sometimes it's a really good thing to be tolerant of other people'.

> Correlating directly with the flâneur's desire for transient and anonymous interactions, Becky describes the comfort that can be drawn from these types of abbreviated and fleeting urban sociabilities: 'You're never alone when you live in the city and I like that. I don't like isolation ... in the city there's always people around, even if they're strangers and anonymous, there are these fleeting possibilities .... It's comforting, it really is. I think it's an odd type of community but I enjoy it'.

This state of co-existence that permits momentary, intimate glances into people's lives became an unintentionally prominent focus throughout my early fieldnotes. I became hooked on capturing that melancholic sensation that seemed to flow as an ever-present undercurrent to daily life in the city. I developed a habit of writing the most intimate things I could observe about the people around me on buses and Tube carriages, often in the form of single words or stand-alone observations.

> Stain on shirt.

> Scar on neck.

> Odd socks.

> I watch her as she soothes her face with a soft, moist wet wipe. I'm close enough to smell its floral scent. She moves the cloth around her face, folds it and repeats. She moves on to her hands, wiping the length of each finger. Her skin is glistening as she wipes herself clean from the dirt of the day. It is intimate, sensuous and made public. There is something comforting about it. I feel relaxed watching her. It's a glimpse into her routine, her personal

life, of the tenderness and self-care that she permits herself. Private in public. A slow moment amidst the rush. (Fieldnotes, 31 March 2017)

Clip on earrings.

Bead of sweat.

Missed a hair shaving.

At the time, these observations often seemed whimsical and futile in terms of actual research, and yet, the implication of these fragmented annotations became clearer to me when I later considered them through the lens of rhythmanalysis. Each of them revealed something about the person I encountered. It exposed their particular and personal rhythms and helped me acknowledge that, despite individual rhythms becoming seemingly entrained by the dominant temporalities of the city and Tube, they remained all the same. Not eradicated but nudged into the background. Recognising the subtle presence of these rhythms decelerated time and disrupted the notion of the rapid city as an entirely dominant and dictating mechanism. It allowed me a discernment of the plurality and complexity of the polyrhythmic interactions that manifest in the city.

The melancholy caused by these brief glimpses into the lives of others, the sense of an ephemeral, anonymous, transitory connection is a privilege only afforded to those living in the modern metropolis, and traditionally, only to men (Elkin, 2016; Wilson, 1991). It is one of the features of the flâneur that holds most dear: detachment; the ability to observe and be observed, without interacting. Alongside the descriptions of strolling and exploring the city for leisure, the pleasure that women attribute to these fleeting interactions perhaps demonstrates that they are indeed embodying certain traits of the flâneur, giving hope to the attainability of the modern day flâneuse. Yet conversely, it takes little imagination to see how the permutation of co-presence, anonymity and transient exchanges can also leave women exposed to less desirable, intrusive and non-consensual interactions. These apparent freedoms will be brought back into debate when women articulate how the risk of sexual harassment acts to disrupt and challenge their negotiations with the city.

Rhythms are also important here as to how women experience the city as a place of comfort and freedom. Knowing a rhythm or becoming accustomed to the rhythmic ensemble of a place is significant.

As Laya states: 'I'm fairly fearless when I travel around London because I know its rhythms. And it really does have its own rhythms'.

Here, adopting the pace of the city and knowing its tempo is described as offering a sense of accomplishment and belonging. This 'knowing' of the city was considered with specific regard to adapting to its spatio-temporal nature.

> Rach, 30, a bartender living in Bristol and travelling to London regularly for work said: 'I still feel excited when I arrive and don't have to check where I'm going, that I'm moving quickly ... there's an excitement and a sense of achievement that you've conquered London'.

As discussed by Lefebvre (2004), the rhythmic ensemble of a space contributes significantly to how it is experienced, and the rhythmical attributes of speed and pace are often considered one of London's defining elements.

> Rach elaborates, saying: 'It's fun and exciting but also exhausting, so I couldn't live here because everything is always open and it's busy busy busy, go go go all the time'. Grace similarly describes the city as having a '24/7 culture ... people are always around and it's constantly going'.

> Alison considered this saying: 'They say in London getting some-where never takes less than 45 minutes, some places take me an hour and a half ... back home in Grimsby you wouldn't travel that far to meet someone for dinner ... it's a weird concept but I quickly got used to it and that's just part of the way of being in London. I don't think about it now'.

This illustrates how time takes on a different quality in relation to space and how these various urban tempos establish the quality of rapidity that is such a dominant rhythm in London. I quickly came to recognise the importance of being acquainted with these temporal rhythms in order to feel settled and at home in the city. In the first few months in London, my fieldnotes and reflexive diary possess a tone of excitement laced with a consistent weariness, as I wrote of the city 'sapping my energy', and of feeling constantly jostled by the crowds and over-whelmed by the fast pace that often left me exhausted, anxious and fragmented. In February, after five months of living in the city, I wrote of arriving back into St Pancras station after a short trip away:

> With a smile I realised that this comforting feeling I was experi-encing was familiarity. The clashing noises and too bright lights in the hall of the station, the repetitive mingling of people arriv-ing, leaving and waiting, the sagging of the seats on the Tube, it all made me feel at ease where before I had felt tension ... and I was no longer thinking about my next move, I was just mov-ing methodically, in a reassuring, arrogant, trance like state ... I feel like I've gradually become intertwined with the city, at times I can't tell if my pace of walking is my own choice or if it's the push and pull of those around me. (Fieldnote extract, 24 February 2017)

I had gradually adapted my own rhythms and movements to those of the city, becoming part of the polyrhythmic ensemble. Similarly, many women, both those who were 'born and bred' in London, and those who have come to know the city as a place called home, described the pleasure in having corporeal knowledge of these urban rhythms, that often led to a perceptual ownership of the streets and public space.

> Kath who recently moved to Leicester, said that she has a 'London walk', which she re-embodies when she 'steps back into London, like a skipping rope'. She described her 'London walk' as 'rude and rapid, speeding and weaving with no eye contact … in London I stride with purpose and ownership wherever I go, I take no prisoners, these are my streets'.

> Grace has lived in the city since she was 18 and similarly described how having a sense of familiarity impacts her attitude towards navigating the city: 'I think there's a bit of arrogance that comes from kind of growing up in London, knowing London … it's my claim to the city'.

This sense of ownership of the streets is derived, at least in part, from implicitly knowing, embodying and performing (consciously or subconsciously) particular dominant rhythms that are present and active in parts of the city. Being accustomed to its complexities and rhythms was significant to women's confidence and conviction in the city, permitting them to experience and act out a version of flânerie.

However, despite the freedom that the dominant rhythms and sociabilities of London can foster, they can also act to induce feelings of fear and isolation. As highlighted in historical literature regarding urban life, the urban public domain was initially perceived as a dangerous and mentally damaging arena, particularly for women (Hubbard, 2012; Massey, 1994). Whilst the contemporary city is now hailed as a desirable and profitable place to live (Zukin, 2009), women highlighted concerns that they pertained as specific to life in the city, particularly feelings of fear, isolation and the relentless pressure of a high-paced life.

> These elements were emphasised by Emmy, 31, who lived in London for a year before moving to a village in the Midlands. She said: 'I wanted to be based in London but it wasn't for me. There were bits I hated, especially the rush and stress of getting the Tube every day. I found it a very isolating place to be and I think I didn't feel that safe'.

A high proportion of depictions of fear and discomfort came from those who did not live in the city. This relates back to the notion that knowledge, familiarity and being accustomed to the rhythms of a place, all contribute to feeling safe, competent and more at ease in the city (Hornsey, 2012).

> Ellie, 30, who travels to London occasionally for work from her home in Brighton recognised this saying: 'London is too hectic for me. I can find it quite fast and frightening and I definitely feel less safe. I'm sure that has a bit to do with it not being my home, with it being unknown, but it can be quite a scary place'.

As well as feelings of fear, a more commonly emphasised notion was that the city was 'hard work'. Whilst for some, the urban temporalities of London created a sense of importance and excitement, others highlighted how this unforgiving rapidity acted to create sociabilities and interactions that led to feelings of isolation.

> Dora, who enjoyed the anonymity of the city, said: 'It can be a harsh place, tough, and incredibly difficult to live in if you're feeling down or not doing so well. When things were not going well for me I felt like the city was just chewing me up and was about to spit me out, it was awful. And when you're down, nobody gives a shit. If you're crying on the tube no one is going to ask you, which is great if you want to be alone but not when you're at a point where you just need somebody to say it's going to be ok. Nobody is going to tell you that, they're going to look away'.

This reveals the conflicting experience of sociabilities in the city: they simultaneously permit anonymity and freedom *and* induce a sense of isolation and loneliness. As a specific, transitory space, the Underground has its own rhythms that implicate women's experiences of mobility in the city, and this is given specific attention below. It helps us to develop an understanding of the network as an arena of abundant mobility, composed of multitudinous rhythms that coalesce to create the atmospheres of the stations, carriages and places in between. The interactions that occur within these liminal spaces, including incidents of sexual harassment, are meaningfully shaped by these rhythms and social atmospheres.

The Need for Speed: Rhythms of the Underground

Simultaneously replicating and facilitating the institutionalised, time-conscious rhythms of the city above, the Underground is a rapid, regular transport network. As a far-reaching mobility system, it is an integral component of life in London, facilitating the everyday mobilisation of bodies around the city. The network is often seen as being dominated by the fast-paced circadian beat of commuters, with an impersonality and insolence that imposes itself (Bissell, 2010). Yet with more intimate observation and analysis, it becomes apparent that there are innumerable rhythms, individual and collective, that concurrently exist and interact in tension with one another. The nature and hierarchy of these rhythms will be explored here, and their impact upon sociabilities on the network will be investigated throughout succeeding chapters.

The necessity of the Underground was emphasised by most participants who lived in London.

> Carla, who has lived, studied and worked in London her whole life said: 'London couldn't function day to day without it … it's vital, and it's amazing that when the system breaks down, you see the city come to a standstill, you really see the effects. It goes to show how important the Underground is for life in the city, work, pleasure or studying, it's absolutely vital to get around.

> Eliza describes it as 'enabling' and said that without it 'your experience, your life in London is stunted'.

> Alison considers how 'it opens everything up and makes the whole city accessible'. And Rachel says how 'life would be so much harder without the convenience of it'.

The network's regularity and predictability were considered to be the system's most defining and favourable features. Each Tube stop has real-time computerised updates that signify when the next train will be arriving, accompanied with regular updates in the form of voice announcements. At peak times, and even off-peak, there is rarely a gap of more than 5–10 minutes between departures, with trains often arriving every 1–3 minutes in central areas of the city.

> Ruth describes her appreciation for how accurately she could calculate her commute when she lived in London: 'I'd leave my house at 7.20, walk for 20 minutes, then the first train would take 26 minutes, then the Waterloo and City Line would take 8 minutes. I did that every day for three years. The convenience was amazing'.

> Comparing London transport to Bristol, Rach says: 'I prefer the Tube. Buses are never on time, or they just don't show up. The Tube … you don't have to wait more than two minutes, and you know it'll be there. That makes it so convenient'.

This illustrates how some of the women have an affinity with the rhythmic attributes that are equated with the modern city. The predictability of the environment was also highlighted as allowing for ease of travel.

> Demi states: 'For people who use it everyday … you don't really need to pay any attention, it's like wallpaper, you're on auto-pilot'.

> Sara, 40, describes how she is 'obsessively routine … I stand in the same spot on the platform because I know where the doors open. It's always the same', and Carla says how she enjoys using

the Tube because 'I don't have to think much ... it's easy to work out, it's not complicated'.

This, in part, signifies the success of Harry Beck's (the creator of the topological Tube map) vision for Tube users to become self-governed and therefore more efficient within a legible environment (Hornsey, 2012). As well as allowing for a maximised use of time, these aspects also permitted a sense of security and safety, particularly at night.

> Sara says: 'the Tube is so consistent and reliable that it makes you feel safe, the familiarity and predictability makes you unconcerned. It's like a cocoon from the streets, it's indoors and regulated'.

> Similarly, Rose considered: 'The Tube is so familiar, why would I be frightened of it ... when something is familiar there's less fear and the Tube is so familiar and reliable, it's always the same. Every time I go on the Tube I have a very similar experience to the last time I was on the Tube'.

These repetitive and predictable experiences are, at least in part, resultant of the Underground's materiality, its architecture and the way the system is physically structured (both the trains themselves, the tunnels, and the stations). It is designed to dictate, or at least encourage a homogenous mode of being. Like the city, rapidity is a dominant rhythm on the Underground. Not just in the mechanical speed of the trains, but equally in the ebb and flow of individual bodies moving as a collective within the network, that are similarly moving to minimise time in transit.

> Annie, whose job as a tutor required her to travel all over the city captures this saying: 'I always feel like I'm in a rush, even when I'm not, on the tube it just always feels like that, maybe because everyone else is rushing. So you're annoyed if you miss a train, even though you have plenty of time and there's another one in two minutes. So often I think it's quite a stressful experience that makes you very aware of time'.

> Demi, who visits regularly for business trips, also describes her movements through the network as dominated by speed: 'On the Underground I'm always moving quite fast, I'm part of the movement, I can't help it, I'm kind of powering through, walking up the escalators and wherever I go I'm looking ahead for the most efficient paths through the crowd without getting in the way of anyone else'.

This prevailing impulse for speed became evident to me when I was riding the Underground purely for the purpose of ethnographic observations (rather than to get somewhere). I was essentially travelling without a destination, and consequently without any real sense of urgency or purpose. And yet I found myself struggling to slow down, and I still felt a twinge of annoyance at missing a train by a millisecond. I was swept up in the seemingly irresistible current of the network, and the urge to harmonise my movements and tempo with those around me. As well as speed, some women considered how, on the Underground, they felt a change in their persona when travelling, particularly at rush hour.

> Ruth says, 'the journey does turn you into an aggressive and confrontational person because everyone else is, it's sort of infectious'.

> Chloe considers: 'I don't think I'm a very nice person on the Tube, I'm rushed and unforgiving, I want to get through'.

> Grace describes how when she embarks upon the part of her commute that is on the Tube: 'I switch and I'm in work mode, I fight to get on, I get more aggressive, I push in and don't let anyone in'.

> Sheila mirrors this saying: 'Sometimes on the Tube I want to lose my temper ... with tourists, when it's rush hour and they're holding you up because they don't know what they're doing at the ticket barriers, you just want to swear at them!'

This has strong connotations with Simmel's (1903) idea that the nature of the metropolis changes individual's behaviour (metropolitan individuality) and Bissell's (2010) consideration of the affective nature of commuting. Often these frustrations were brought out by disruptions to the normative, fast-paced rhythms:

> Kreeda says: 'You should know which direction you're going in, and always have your Oyster card ready at the gates because otherwise that holds people up and you can create a back log that stops the flow of people going'.

> Similarly, Cris, who often travels in rush hour says: 'You get your card ready, the barriers can slow you down but it should be easy, you tap your card down and that's usually quite smooth but you get annoyed at people when they aren't as ready as you'.

> Ruth, remembering her first few weeks commuting in London says: 'If for some reason you've not got your ticket ready, you want the ground to swallow you up because you know you're holding people up, even if it's a nanosecond, it's just the awkwardness of having to take that step backwards ... you learn to try and avoid it'.

Many of these norms, described by Tess as 'Tube etiquette', are so ubiquitous because they actively contribute to the flow of people and thus, capital, through the system. Signage, posters and audio announcements from Transport for London and British Transport Police are regular features around the network, often in an explicit attempt to manage subjects that move through the system by signifying preferential modes of behaviour. For example, this includes instructions to stand on the right side of the escalator to let people move quickly on the left, to move down into the middle of carriages to make more space, to let people off the carriages before getting on, and to have your ticket or oyster card ready when approaching the barriers. Yet despite 'official' instruction, much of the corporeal movement that can be observed when moving through the network is embodied and self-governed by regular users of the Tube. From my observations, I recorded countless incidents of passengers regulating and disciplining one another's behaviour if it was not deemed appropriate. The following fieldnote was recorded within a few weeks of me arriving in London:

> It's 9.45 pm at St Pancras. Walking through the passageway from the Underground to the main station, the flow of people moves swift and purposefully. Polished heels are clicking, and trench coats are swirling in the gust of the tunnel. As I move with the stream of bodies, I notice (or feel?) a disruption. A man who has just marched past me pushes by another man who is walking (relatively) slowly; he responds by exclaiming 'Woah, scuse me mate!' The first man looks back without stopping and says 'You are in the way, you shouldn't be walking in the middle, walk to the side if you're going so slowly', to which the second man replies: 'I don't have the same control over how fast I walk as you do'. At closer observation, it becomes clear that he is hobbling slightly, walking with a slight limp. The older (faster) man waves his hand dismissively in the air behind him, and that is the end of their exchange. (Fieldnote extract, October 2016)

This epitomises how users of the Underground discipline one another into conforming to the social norms and rhythms of space. It also signifies how individual bodily, physiological rhythms can serve as a disruption to the collective. At the time, I felt indignant towards the first man for his rudeness and hostility. Yet only a few weeks later, I had Canadian friends visiting, and (to my shame) felt a fluttering of anxiety in my stomach as they stood obtrusively on the left-hand side of the escalator and chatted loudly and cheerfully across the aisle on a busy Tube carriage. I didn't *want* to feel embarrassed, but ... they were breaking the rules! I had to consciously stop myself from glancing apologetically at fellow travellers. My internalisation of the social norms of the Underground was mirrored by some of the women, but they described how they took pride in calling people out if they were acting in a way that was deemed inappropriate for the space. This included telling other passengers to take off backpacks, to move down the carriages and to give up seats for elderly people or pregnant women. This pervasive (social) policing of others demonstrates how dominant rhythms and modes of behaviour are established, embodied and (re)enforced.

In her work on the embodiment of urban geographies, Middleton (2010) discusses the practice of being a 'good' or 'skilled' pedestrian in London. Here, women expressed similar sentiments of pride in being established and competent Tube users.

Alongside whole bodily movements, there are also 'micro' behaviours that are collectively enacted within the space of the Underground. These interactions are ones that, whilst seemingly unfriendly and antisocial, are often deemed as necessary and appropriate for the efficient functioning of a system that requires such a high level of co-presence. Two of the most iterated examples of this were a pervading silence, and a lack of eye contact on carriages.

> When I asked women to describe the 'social scene' of the Underground these aspects came up repeatedly: 'It's a very formal and British space, so no eye contact, little speech and even smiling is somewhat frowned upon as being too intimate' (Sammi); 'zero eye contact, and I can probably count the number of conversations I've heard on the tube' (Alison); and, 'avoid eye contact and keep to yourself'. (Sara)

Despite their functionality, some women felt that these combined sociabilities meant the Tube was an immensely unpleasant, impersonal and stressful place.

> Eliza and Emmy both described rush hour as 'survival of the fittest' and Ruth, who noted the Underground as one of the main reasons she left London said: 'It's the worst part of anyone's day, it's miserable everyone just wants to get to work so they can carry on being a normal human being ... when I could, I'd avoid the Underground at all costs'.

> Yet most of the women I spoke to recognised the function of these seemingly hostile norms as a way of 'allowing people their personal space whilst really, there is absolutely none' (Kreeda). Sammi also says: 'a lot of it is about allowing people to stay in their private bubbles'.

In fact, some women spoke of how the rhythms of the Underground, and the anonymous interactions they induce, allow a sense of comfort and pleasure whilst on the move, that can be paralleled to the activity of the flâneuse. Whilst (if she existed at all) she traditionally roamed the city on foot, these accounts reveal that fragments of the character of the elusive flâneuse are being embodied and experienced on the Underground.

> Rose hints at this saying: 'I can be completely disconnected from everybody else, and that's allowed in this space, there's no obligation for me to interact with people'.

This pleasure in transit connects with Goffman's (1963) concept of 'allocation involvement', whereby travelling is the main purpose and activity being performed, thereby permitting the opportunity to withdraw and relax.

> Alison also captures the possibility of being alone in the crowd, saying: 'My commute is an hour and twenty minutes long, but I love it! It's a bit of me time that I rarely get ... nobody talks to me, it's silent on the Tube which I love. I don't get a moment to myself so sometimes I'll make my journey home extended so I have more time on public transport ... even though you're surrounded by so many people, that's my alone time'.

> Grace said that she finds being on the Tube 'comforting and relaxing'. And Rachel explained that when she was writing her Ph.D. she would 'sometimes get my laptop out and sit on the circle line and go round and round, I found it a relaxing environment to write in, I think because it was insulated from the outside world'.

> Becky said: 'It's a place where no one expects anything of you, it's almost like being at home because no one expects anything of you, you can just go about what you need to do, put your headphones in ... when you're travelling nothing is expected of you. Because I'm working and studying, I don't get any down time and 40 minutes, twice a day I can listen to a podcast, I don't have to talk to anybody, nobody needs anything from me, I don't have to think about anything, I don't have to process any information, it's my quiet time. I think for a lot of people in London that's the same'.

> Chloe describes her commute in a similar fashion: 'Once I get on it's my own personal space, a really key part of my day, I read my book, zone out or whatever. It's often the only time of the day where no one is interacting with me, it's alone time, relaxing before I get catapulted into my job'.

This mirrors research that has acknowledged the positive utility of commuting time (Redmond & Mokhtarian, 2001) and framed it as desirable time to oneself or, 'me time', in a separate 'third space' between work and home (Pindek et al., 2023). There are also enjoyable moments on the Tube when the veneer of 'hostility' is broken.

> Rose describes these fleeting moments saying: 'I've actually had some really nice experiences on the Tube, small chats and little smiles when you catch someone's eye. And those moments can make you feel good'.

Laya further explores this, explaining: 'You sometimes get those moments where something happens and it unites the whole carriage, everyone laughs, it breaks down that shield, only briefly but when you see it happen you realise, the barriers everyone puts up on the Tube, it's deliberate but it can be broken easily, it's a temporary and fragile construct'.

As a fundamental part of London life, the Underground, acting as the veins and arteries of the city, can often be seen as mono-rhythmic, relentless and hostile. Indeed, the network is structured and managed in order to encourage fast and efficient movement and it is clear that these notions of predictability and efficiency act to create a sense of ontological security. Yet with more intimate observation and analysis it becomes apparent that there are innumerable rhythms, individual and collective, that concurrently exist and generally interact in relative harmony. These can even be experienced as comforting, offering women the opportunity to engage in a contemporary form of flânerie. Yet despite the curation of this space in which freedom can be felt, it will become apparent when looking at incidents of sexual harassment on the network that the accumulation of these rhythms and the behavioural norms they define, are all significant in shaping the trajectory of incidents of sexual harassment that happen within the space. The following section will explore how (the threat of) sexual harassment more broadly constitutes a part of and a disruption to these rhythms and women's lives in the city.

Disruption on the Line: The Risk and Anticipation of Male Violence

[...] expect it and then accept it. (Janice)

Despite women displaying and enacting forms of modern day flânerie and discussing how the city and the Underground provided them with freedom, anonymity and pleasure, they also spoke of how the risk and actuality of sexual harassment and men's intrusions impacted their negotiations of the city and how they experienced public space.

Grace, who spoke strongly about her feelings of ownership of the streets considered: 'I do feel I have access to everything in London. But I will say that with that comes a constant reassurance to myself that I have this access, rather than it just being, I have to reassure myself ... I have a place here, I can do this ... it's like this internal monologue that just takes up headspace. I really want to get to the point where it doesn't enter my head'.

Chloe expresses similar sentiments about navigating the possibility of unwanted interactions with men in public, saying: 'Having to think about these things ... it's an invasion of your mental space', and Eliza, considers: 'Worrying about these things is annoying because it kind of distracts you from your personal zoning out time'.

One of the core characteristics of the flâneur is his ability to be aimless and aloof whilst traversing the city. Whilst the previous sections of this chapter show many women enjoy the practice of urban wandering, the perceived risk of male violence insists that they maintain a sense of vigilance. Furthermore, many of the women recognise the gendered nature of this tension as something that men are often oblivious to.

Janice summarises this saying that sexual harassment: 'for most men it's just not in their sphere of expectation. For women we almost expect it and then accept it'. Gillian spoke about how her male friends are always surprised and disbelieving when she recounts stories of sexual harassment.

Similarly, Ally says: 'I find it frustrating that men have no idea what it's like, and so they're so dismissive of sexual harassment because they've never been followed home, they've never had someone expose themselves, shouted at. Men don't understand that it isn't a one off, these are regular, multiple experiences'.

Demi talked about how when she spoke to male colleagues about sexual harassment in public space they saw it as a joke, and she said 'it's not a joke. You don't know what it's like to have to watch yourself all the time'.

In this sense, the fear or knowledge of the potential for sexual harassment is an active and ever present normative (psychological) rhythm that women navigate. Furthermore, as well as being a psychological rhythm, it often manifests in physical actions in order to traverse public space in a way that feels safe.

Demi said: 'You're forever having to justify that you want to exist in public space without harassment, so I think we all have these little things we do to protect ourselves, ask any of my female friends, they'll tell you'.

Kath considers how: 'It doesn't matter where you go, there's always this other layer of navigation, like you're constantly policing yourself and your actions'.

Tara mentions having 'safety plans' to get home at night, and Laya considers the exhaustion from occupying these thoughts: 'it's bullshit that we have to continually come up with these like, tactics and negotiations to feel safe in public space'.

These strategies and negotiations caused by the risk of sexual harassment and violence act to demonstrate that whilst women are an equal part of the urban scene, experiences of the city's public spaces remain highly gendered and often fraught with challenges.

Despite the omnipresent and normalised risk of sexual harassment that many women experience and internalise, when an incident does occur, it still causes 'arrhythmia' and a disruption to a general sense of safety and well-being, often causing feelings of vulnerability, distress and anger, and making the city (temporarily) seem an unfamiliar and intimidating place.

> Speaking of an incident of sexual harassment she experienced, Sammi states: 'It really shook me up, I was always aware of dangers, but it came out of nowhere. I was in my own little world, and it came like a slap in the face'.

> Tara describes this similarly saying: 'Every time something like this happens, even a little thing, it sort of rocks you and wakes you up'.

> Kath considers: 'The most violating thing was that it was challenging to my idea that I was free to go about my business as I please without interruption'.

These comments reveal that women's daily trajectories in the city require a level of negotiation in public space that, largely, does not exist for men. Discussions about women's access (and limits) to public urban space have been historically situated within discourses of vulnerability, often taking on a highly paternalistic nature. This remains pervasive (if more subtle) in modern society and was recognised and challenged by some of the women who explicitly demanded the right to take risks. As Phadke et al. (2011, p. 180) consider, by doing so 'we are implicitly rejecting this conditional protection in favour of the unqualified right to public space'.

> Chloe speaks about this explicitly: 'I feel for a really long time people have been frightened about travelling around on their own as a woman and I don't like that. It's really important to me that it's not a big deal. I don't like it when people say let me know you get home safe ... there should be no reason to expect that I won't. I won't live like that'.

> Ally expresses similar sentiments: 'I tend to get angry when people say oh don't walk home alone, these things could happen to you. And I'm like I know, you think I don't know this? But what annoys me is it shouldn't be this way, why are you conditioning me to be afraid, reinforcing this behaviour, making it acceptable to say I shouldn't go out on my own? That pisses me off'.

These reflections show that traversing the city in an aimless and uninhibited way, is a prospect that exists just out of reach in contemporary London. Whilst many women highlighted that the city provides them with a sense of freedom, anonymity and pleasure, the perceived risk and anticipation of gendered violence exist as a tension and limitation to these experiences. The perceived need to assess and negotiate one's presence and safety in urban space is pervasive. Yet looking at this through the lens of the flâneur allows us to challenge narratives that *only* present the danger, fear and victimisation that women experience in urban space. Reaching optimistically for the possibility of the flâneuse forces us to engage with the multitudinous rhythms and negotiations women occupy when navigating the city.

This chapter has offered a tapestry of women's experiences that 'set the scene', or the 'before', everyday stage, amidst which incidents of sexual harassment on the London Underground play out. Using Lefebvre's rhythmanalysis and the concept of the flâneur, this chapter has portrayed the tensions that exist with the possibility of a claim for the modern day flâneuse in London. These accounts given by women come together to co-create a representation of the rhythmic attributes of the city and the Underground, and how they impact urban experience. Finally, these themes were drawn together to demonstrate how the anticipation and perceived risk of sexual harassment, both constitute women's normative rhythms *and* act as disruptions that hinder their perceived freedom in the city. As we see in the following chapter, these anticipations are not misplaced, as the urban rhythms and sociabilities we have explored here are exploited in the spaces and paces of the Underground.

Chapter 5

'During': Moments of Sexual Harassment on the London Underground

Abstract

This chapter focusses on the 'during' – the actual corporeal experiences of sexual harassment on the London Underground. I explore these 'moments' in detail, the nitty gritty complexity of these experiences that often hold vulnerability, fear, resistance, anger and ambivalence all at once. As considered above, this 'messiness' can be lost in quantitative work, to the detriment of a nuanced understanding of sexual harassment. I continue to explore and understand these moments through the lens of mobility, again operationalising Lefebvre's *rhythmanalysis* and Cresswell's (2010) concept of *friction* in order to draw out key conceptual observations that are specific to how sexual harassment manifests in a public transport environment. Using a framework that has movement and mobilities at its core, this chapter links sexual harassment to spatial and temporal elements of the broader city and its transport system. In doing so, it shows how these multiple rhythms coalesce to create the conditions within which sexual harassment is perpetrated and experienced in a certain and particular way. The framework illustrates how harassment is, in part spatially implicated, facilitated or hindered by the spaces and paces of the city.

Keywords: Sexual harassment; public transport; London Underground; mobilities; rhythmanalysis

Mind the Gender Gap: A Mobilities Perspective of Sexual Harassment on the
London Underground, 75–94
doi:10.1108/978-1-83753-026-720241005

Railway stations and trains are '… places of unexpected social inter-change as people's lives from distant parts are contingently brought together, often only for 'brief encounters' before the characters move away'. (Urry, 2007, p. 109)

When it first happened, when he first started rubbing himself against me, I didn't really realise what was happening. There are a lot of people on there and he did it in time with the swaying of the tube carriage …. By the time I really realised, like properly, what was going on, that he was actually rubbing against me, it was too late because it was my stop. (Demi)

The overarching aim of this chapter is to identify the key features of experiences of sexual harassment in a transport environment. At this part of the journey, we slow down time, and zoom in, to focus on the 'during' – the actual, corporeal moments of these intrusions. I explore these 'moments' in detail, to draw out and give credence to the complexities and contradictions that they hold. By doing this, we see that these experiences often induce feelings of vulnerability, fear, confusion, resistance, anger and ambivalence (sometimes all at once), shaping women's immediate reactions to these intrusions and assaults. We continue to look at these experiences through the lens of mobility, again operationalising Lefebvre's rhythmanalysis and Cresswell's (2010) concept of friction to highlight key conceptual observations that are specific to how sexual harassment manifests in a public transport environment. Using a framework that has movement and mobilities at its core, this chapter links sexual harassment to spatial and temporal elements of the broader city and its transport system. In doing so, it shows how these multiple rhythms coalesce to create the conditions within which sexual harassment is perpetrated and experienced in a certain and particular way.

By taking this approach, I identify three key conceptual observations that constitute unique features of sexual harassment on public transport. These have been discussed elsewhere (Lewis et al., 2021), and I take this opportunity to review these characteristics in more detail and show how they manifest in women's in-depth accounts. To begin, the rhythms of the city above permeate the Underground, and are used by perpetrators to *aid* and *conceal* sexual harassment in different ways, at varying times of the day. Bissel (2009) considers how travelling by train is often characterised by the density of strangers being transported in proximity. As we explored in the previous chapter, this is most recognisable in morning and evening rush hours. At these times, passengers are restrained on platforms and in carriages with one another – physical contact is common and largely understood as an unavoidable norm. The density of people allows certain types of sexual harassment to be perpetrated, most notably in the form of groping and frotteuring, in a way that remains relatively hidden. As we will see in Ruth and Sheila's stories, offenders act within the normative, rhythmic, composition of the busy carriage without *observably* transgressing the social norms of the space. They surreptitiously exploit the high level of interpersonal tactility within the space to perpetrate and obscure their assaults. In the stories below, we will also see how perpetrators used the rhythms of the urban and the Underground to stalk through the network in a non-suspicious way (see Rach's account), and to perpetrate blatantly sexual behaviour when the carriages are isolated at quiet, off-peak times or in more remote areas of the city (see Grace and Carla's accounts). This obfuscation often defines incidents of harassment in these mobile spaces, causing confusion and subsequent distress for victims as they are forced to navigate these intrusions that are shrouded in uncertainty.

The second key conceptual observation is that the strict, normative social rules of the Tube are implicit in curbing women's responses to sexual harassment. The rhythmic flow of movement through the Tube network shows regulated bodies coming together to move as a 'polyrhythmic' (Lefebvre, 2004) collective. Horn-sey (2012, p. 686) describes how the Underground is designed to function with 'the logic of a factory assembly line' and Urry (2007, p. 38) posits that, this is in part constituted by the fact that 'people know how to behave on the move'. Consequently, anything that creates a disruption or *friction* to people's journeys is often treated with contempt (Edensor, 2011). As Lefebvre writes on 'dressage', he discusses the disciplining and training of the body. Physiological bodily rhythms coexist with and are conditioned by the social environment, as we train ourselves and are trained to behave according to the norms of the space (Lefebvre, 2004). This is interesting to consider when women are anxious about reacting overtly due to breaking the social etiquette of the Tube. He describes how we contain ourselves by concealing the diversity of our rhythms, stating 'humans break themselves in like animals. They learn to hold themselves' (Lefebvre, 2004, p. 48). This acts as a form of friction, as women may *feel* a certain way (fear, anger, etc.), yet often act in a way that is against their own rhythms in order to conform to the space in which the body is situated. As discussed previously, one of the most observable interactions on the Tube is Goffman's (1963) concept of 'civil inattention', a deference owed to strangers in a crowded public space. Whilst essential for survival in the modern city, the women's stories presented here show how collective civil inattention breeds an unsympathetic and isolating environment, diminishing a sense of individual or communal responsibility. This is exacerbated by the prevalence of the 'metropolitan individuality' and the 'blasé outlook' (Simmel, 1903), where excessive stimuli in the city means that 'people are forced to develop an attitude of reserve and insensitivity to feeling' (Urry, 2007, p. 22).

The impact of civil inattention will be given more attention in this chapter. When women recognise that they are being sexually assaulted or harassed, the anxiety that exists around breaching the social etiquette of the Underground and the risk of (by speaking out) causing tension between passengers significantly shapes their responses to these intrusions. As detailed in women's stories below, each of them expressed a reluctance to rebuke their harasser in a confrontational way. Their apprehensions revolved around the risk of humiliation, and the concern that other passengers would treat them with contempt. In conjunction with this, I show how we can further understand this collective apathy of the Tube carriage by drawing on Baumgartner's (1988) concept of 'moral minimalism'. Though her work revolves around the social order of the suburbs, and how conflict is largely avoided here, many elements of this can be transferred to understanding the dynamics of the Tube that are fundamental in shaping women's experiences of sexual harassment. This is not surprising, as Baumgartner suggests moral minimalism is likely to prevail anywhere where there is 'social fluidity, in which people are highly mobile, both physically and inter-personally, and move in and out of relationships constantly' (p. 129). As a place of abundant mobility, moral minimalism is rife within the Tube network. A key example of how this manifests includes understanding the general lack of bystander response when women do not overtly react (for reasons explored below), or as Baumgartner (1988, p. 56) suggests: 'the seriousness of an offense is defined in practice by the response to it. Where moral minimalism prevails, offenses are apt to appear trivial to an observer precisely because their victims react with such restraint'.

The third key conceptual observation is that as a highly peripatetic space, the transitory nature of the Underground often creates a situation where women barely fully register an incident of harassment before it has passed, or they anticipate that it will be over quickly. It also contributes to the perception that perpetrators can swiftly disappear into the network without a trace. As the opening quote from Urry (2007, p. 109) considers, interactions in transport environments are usually 'brief encounters' between strangers. We see this play out in the stories below, where women struggle to comprehend (or believe) what is happening to them before it is over. If they do realise 'in the moment', the transitory nature of the Tube means women often come to a decision not to overtly engage on the basis that their journey and current situation are temporary and will soon come to an end. On top of this, in the context of being in transit, women's priorities are habitually occupied by wanting to get to their destination. We can apply Goffman's (1963) concept of 'allocation involvement' here, to understand how, in transport spaces, people on the move have the primary desire to arrive at their destination, without disruption or ancillary interactions and involvements. Thus, women enact a resistance to the friction caused by harassment: in many instances, they refuse to slow down and to let their mobilities be disrupted. Concurrent to this, it is important to consider how perpetrators operate amidst the transience and anonymity that shrouds the network and use this atmosphere to almost seamlessly 'slip away' after they have perpetrated their assaults. In these circumstances, the perpetual motion of both trains and individuals constructs the illusion that the offender has disappeared and is untraceable amongst the spaces and paces of the Underground. The rest of the chapter will show the manifestation of each of these conceptual observations through women's descriptions of their experiences of 'concealment', 'etiquette' and 'brief encounters'.

Concealment

> *She said she was standing, holding on to one of the poles so she didn't lurch forwards and backwards with the movement of the carriage, which she knew was about to stop. It was a crowded, morning rush hour, arms everywhere, bodies close together. Nothing particularly unusual for her commute into the city. As the train began to brake,*

screeching to a sluggish stop, she felt a firm, tough hand grabbing her waist. She said she froze, muscles tensing, surprised by the sudden physical contact and the purposefulness of it – different from the usual brushing and accidental bumps that are bound to happen with so many people in a confined space. A moment later, she felt another hand on her other side, again a strong grab. The hands stayed there for a second, and then, as the train jolted to a standstill, forcibly moved her to one side and a man in a suit nudged past her. She asked me 'is that sexual harassment?' I didn't know how to answer, so I asked her if she thought it was. She didn't know. He could have said excuse me, she said. He didn't need to touch me. Maybe it wasn't sexual, but it was unnecessary and inappropriate. She said she felt intimidated. Confused. It felt intrusive, but did he really do anything wrong? (Reflections on an informal conversation with Beth, 11 November 2016).

Lefebvre (2004) argues that the rhythms of the city are, above all, dominated by the flow of capital and productivity: the mechanisms of daily grind. In London, this is most observable during 'rush hours' in the central areas of the city. It is at this time-space axis where the infamous stereotype of Tube travel manifests, with agitated commuters wedged up against each other on platforms and carriages in order to maximise flow and efficiency, both on an individual and collective level within the network. It takes little conjecture to see how this physical and social dynamic is exploited to perpetrate incidents of sexual harassment and assault such as inappropriate and ambiguous touching (like Beth's story above) and frotteuring, or groping. This is the context in which Ruth, whose story we now follow, was assaulted. Her daily commute took place in inner-city London, starting at Waterloo and finishing at Bank, one of the busiest Underground stations located within the City of London (the central business and financial district). This is important, as here, the rhythms of the city above, dictate the rhythms of the Underground. Considering the interaction between the spatial and temporal, Ruth's journey on the Tube is influenced significantly by the fact she is travelling within the heart of the city, on a popular commuter route, at peak time. Overcrowding in the morning rush hours, between 7.30 a.m. and 9.30 a.m., is caused by the mass, daily influx of commuters and, like most transport systems, the Tube is regulated in a way that aims to maximise the speed of those moving through it. Lefebvre (2004, p. 43) encourages us to try and discern a hierarchy amongst the 'tangled mess' of rhythms, to observe and feel whether there is a 'determining rhythm'. In this space, at this time, the dominant rhythm is the corporate rush of the city above, with the Underground facilitating and supplying the city with its workers.

Ruth described how, like every other weekday morning, she was wedged between strangers in a busy rush hour carriage: 'I'd just gotten on to the tube, I hadn't been one of the first people on, I'd been one of the last, so I was standing closer to the doors, you know that shut behind you, almost on you. And there were lots of people around me and at some point during that 8 minutes, I felt someone's hand touch me really closely, on my pubic bone. It was done in a way that, you know when you're a child and you need the toilet and you might cup yourself, it was that motion. So, somebody had gone in with the tips of their fingers and palm up and gone underneath .... And the bizarre thing is that it happened so quickly, and there didn't appear to be anybody that looked as though it was obviously them. Because getting the Waterloo and City into Bank means that the majority of people on that carriage are men, and they're suited and booted working men usually sort of between 30 and 50 years old and it could have been anyone. I couldn't tell the angle of where the hand was coming from so it could have been the bloke to my right or my left, or slightly to the side, I just didn't know, and everyone was just looking around like normal, and I was going, is this really happening? But the hand was still there. It must have stayed there for maybe 5 seconds. And it moved, but then I just sort of felt a finger move from side to side like a pendulum on my pubic bone, and then it went and then the tube arrived, and the doors opened, and everyone got off'.

Ruth intrinsically ties the movements of urbanity to her personal experience. The way in which she reflects on her assault highlights how the broader rhythms of the city and the Underground network become corporeally felt on an intimate level. She also notes how, despite the understanding that personal space is limited on the Tube, and thus, physical contact is to be expected, the interaction described above still felt instantly jarring:

And this happened and at first I was like .... you're used to people being in your personal space, you're used to people touching you out of necessity, the tops of your arms, your back, your chest, your belly, your bum even, you're just used to being pressed up against people. But I was like there's no way that this is accidental .... It made me feel ... the first thing was shock and disbelief, did that really happen, and you think, it definitely did because I felt it and it must have been deliberate. You question whether anyone would do that on purpose, cos you sort of think did that happen? Yes it did. Could that have been an accident? No it wasn't.

This reminded me of my own experience on the metrobus in Istanbul – I was simultaneously *certain* that I was being assaulted, and, in the same breath, questioning whether it was *really* happening. Ruth's story illustrates how the rhythms of the Underground both enabled and disguised the intrusion of her body and space enough to add an element of confusion and left her navigating a state of obscurity. Within the frenetic hustle of morning rush hours and the temporary physical immobility forced on individuals in the carriages, the movements required to commit this assault deviated in an almost imperceptible way from the 'correct or regular movements of the daily commute' (Cresswell, 2010, p. 25). What this means, is that these digressions are invisible to bystanders and even cause victims to question their own bodily knowledge of what is *really* happening.

> Sheila describes a similar experience implicated by the busyness of the network on an early summer weekend: 'So, I was stood up by the double doors at the back of the carriage and I was kind of, vaguely paying attention to who was getting on and off, and I remember there being this guy who was creepy … I noticed him because he looked out of place. He'd got a big coat on which was a bit strange, given that it was the end of May, and it was red hot out. So, I remember thinking why has he got a coat on, because it's boiling in the carriage. So, I was just standing there sweating and holding on to the pole, and I could see him looking at me, and it makes you a bit neurotic, I think because I'd already been in an abusive relationship, I was a bit wary of men at that stage anyway but not enough to immediately suspect that something was going to happen. And people kept getting on and the carriage was getting quite crowded, and he kept moving closer towards me, and I remember thinking this is getting a bit creepy now, because there's enough room for him to not be that close to me. And he was staring at me and all sweaty, it was really horrible … he was really freaking me out at that stage. I think the stop I was going to get off at was Hammersmith, but I think about quarter of the way through the journey, he was so close to me that I could feel his breath on my face and then he starts basically rubbing on me, this is the bit I find awkward talking about, he had a hard on and he was rubbing it on me. But because it was so crowded in there I couldn't immediately … I think in my head I was thinking it was a bag or an umbrella or something because nobody would do that would they? And he was stood behind me at this stage rubbing on my leg and my bum. I think this carried on for about 5 minutes before I thought oh shit. And I think it's a very English thing to not want to make a fuss even if someone is dry humping you on the tube. I don't know why, I think I was just frightened, you know I don't want to make a fuss'.

Like in Ruth's story, we hear Sheila describe how the offender uses the rhythms of the space to evoke enough ambiguity that she questioned what was happening and therefore did not respond in an overt way. The perpetrator blends in with the composition of the crowd and synchronises with the movement of the carriage, without visibly transgressing from the normative way of behaving in the space. The expected amount of tactile friction that occurs between passengers is exploited to perpetrate and camouflage these incidents of sexual assault. What we see then, is how this weaponising of rhythms generates a (psychological) liminal state between knowing and not knowing that obfuscates women's understandings and reactions, rendering them even more invisible and misunderstood. It is this type of behaviour happening in rush hour carriages that is arguably the 'image' that comes to mind when discussing sexual harassment on public transport, and indeed, many of the stories shared took on some version of this. Yet the 'tactics' used to perpetrate sexual harassment and assault shift significantly depending on circadian temporalities. Another clear exploitation of the (slower) rhythms of the city and the Tube includes perpetrators enacting overtly sexual behaviour when women occupy spaces of the network that are isolated (removed from the urban centre) at 'off-peak' (non-commuter rush hour) travel times.

In Grace's story below, she reflects vividly on an incident that happened when she was 14 years old. It was a weeknight, and she was travelling home from an after-school club on an empty, off-peak Tube, traversing the outskirts of the city. With significantly fewer people and a relative slowness, these interacting rhythms of sub-urban areas create an atmosphere that impresses upon the social interactions occurring within the Tube. Grace spoke of how Upminster station has a noticeably different feel to it in comparison to congested areas, where Londoners appear ambivalent, even repugnant towards one another (Simmel, 1903). Here, people notice each other and brief, even momentary interactions with strangers are not uncommon.

> Grace describes her experience: 'At this time, there was like, no one on the tube. This is the district line. So until I got to the second from last carriage there was no one. And when I got to the second to last carriage, there was a guy standing in the doorway, the doors were still open. I looked at him and he looked at me and I didn't think anything of it. I got on the tube, sat there for a bit. And I either had a blazer or my bag on my lap or something, and I remember sitting there and something about it made me feel wrong already because it was empty apart from me and this one bloke, but I was going two stops and then I was going home, it was a journey I'd done a million times. And then the doors shut and we move off. So we're going to the first stop. And I looked, and through the interconnecting doors, he's looking at me through the window. So that made me feel really intimidated. And he was just staring at me. I remember just staring at my bag, not wanting to engage but needing to know what was happening. I look back and he's still there and then I look back and he's gone, and I thought, weirdo, or whatever. Get to the first stop and no one gets on but he gets off his carriage and gets on to my carriage .... So he's sitting there and I'm thinking ok this is really weird, but you have one stop to go. How long can that take? Well apparently, it takes a really long time! Because as we pull off, I can hear his belt go and I had to kind of look because again I had to see what was happening. And I could see that to me it looked like he was tucking himself in. And I thought that's ok, fine. And then I was sitting there thinking that then he must've sort of moved or something

and I thought you're going to get flashed, that's the first thing that came into my head, you're going to get flashed, prepare yourself, you're going to get flashed. And he never came near me. But I could hear him, and I looked out of the corner of my eye and he was masturbating. And I just had to sit there and just wait until I got to my stop. And then when we got there and the doors opened, what's strange is I went out of the door that was nearest him ... I don't know what that was! I think it must've been like I needed to know if this had actually happened, it was so beyond. I was like am I making this up? And I just stood on the platform like did that just actually happen to me? I stood there for a good few minutes processing it, like trying to figure out did I make it up, was that really happening? Had I gone into some sort of dream? Nothing felt real, it felt quite surreal'.

At the beginning of this interaction, Grace feels uneasy, but can't place why. Some explanations may hint towards a 'gut feeling' or a fear response (de Becker, 2000). However, the rhythms and social norms of the space can also offer an explanation here. The man's initial interaction with Grace was *almost* within the realm of what might be understood as 'normal' between strangers in a public space (an incidental glance, followed by looking away) – this would fall under the 'rules' of 'civil inattention'. However, by holding her gaze, he transgressed the boundary of normative social etiquette enough to make Grace feel uncomfortable. Like in the experiences of sexual harassment in rush hours, obscurity and concealment pervade the entire interaction (both his mode of offending and Grace's response). To a bystander, his extremely predatory actions would likely be indiscernible. He did not talk to Grace or touch her physically, sitting away from her in the carriage. As such, in many ways, he did not break the nonrepresentational modes of interaction that are usual on public transport (Bissell, 2010).

Carla's story has similarities to Grace's: 'I was sitting on the train, heading out to Zone 4, the carriage was pretty much empty, there was probably 4 or 5 people a way down, and opposite me on a seat a bit more to the right, there was a guy sitting there and he had a laptop case on his lap, which he then put in-between his feet, and then he decided to pull his genitals out from his trousers and started masturbating in front of me and I just felt so awkward. I was 17, I was by myself. You don't exactly go up to the person and say hey what are you doing because you don't know how he's going to react. And because it was pretty much empty in the part of the carriage that we were in, it wasn't as if anybody else saw. So I couldn't even go up to anybody else and say you know, would you mind if I sit with you please, I'm feeling a bit uncomfortable about what this guy is doing. But you know I looked at this guy in his face and he looked at me and he just carried on. It was really ... yeah, he had no shame, he was quite brazen in what he was doing ... he was playing with his genitals in front of me. Yeah, it was about 4 minutes to my stop and I stayed, and when you're in that situation at the time, you don't think, like oh my god let me get off the train, you just think oh my god this is happening in a public place'.

Situated within the urban geographies and rhythms of the city and Underground, Carla's harasser was facilitated and concealed by isolation, containment and mobility on the carriage. Whilst his behaviour was explicit and visible to Carla (so she did not have the same uncertainty as Grace), it was concealed from other passengers, and thus constrained scope for responding. Rach's story is slightly different. She talks about her experience of being assaulted and then followed on the Tube network. Travelling in from Bristol for a work night out in London, she is heading back to her sister's house.

I get to Mile End, happily, listening to my podcast. Got to the Mile End tube station and was looking at what train I needed to get because I still wasn't very aware of where I was going, just knew I needed to go West. And that's when I remember ... in the next few minutes I don't remember that much, I just remember flashes because I was relatively drunk but I remember there was someone standing next to the board that said the stops. There was a group of maybe three of them, all men and they were talking to me and implied they'd help me to get home. I thought they were just being kind, having fun. And I don't know if I told them where I was going, I don't think I did but maybe I did. Then all I remember was lips on my lips and I remember putting my hand in-between them and pushing him off. And then he went for me again and I pushed him off again and I remember running down the steps and throwing myself on the first tube. And it was when I was on the tube that everything became really clear, I snapped into, fuck, what just happened. And then I remember looking up and I saw a yellow t-shirt, that's the one thing I recognised about this man, he was wearing a bright yellow t-shirt and was sitting opposite me on the tube .... In hindsight, I should have found the nearest person and said I think I'm being followed but what happens if I'm wrong? The minute we got into Bank, I threw myself off the train, through the tube station very quickly, got on the next tube and sat down and looked up and there he was again in the bright yellow shirt. And that's the main thing I remember, bright yellow shirt. And I thought I can't go to Mornington Crescent because I know how quiet it is and I felt like I needed to be where people are, I need to get above ground. So, I got off at Euston and go upstairs, trying to phone my boyfriend. And then I saw him again, the man who'd followed me, in the bright yellow shirt. He approached me and said are you ok? So, I just turned my back on him because I didn't know what else to do. I went outside, on the phone and he still followed me. I ran and jumped in a taxi and burst into tears.

Rach's harasser first takes advantage of her need to stop and check where she is going (as well as abusing the more relaxed 'night-time' sociabilities of the Tube that will be discussed below). As a 'non-Londoner' her 'urban competency' and mental map of her journey are less established, and the initial interaction is initiated under the guise of 'helping' her. He also uses the network to follow her inconspicuously – whilst his behaviour gradually becomes overt and visible to her (and thus, frightening), his actions are concealed to bystanders by their normality within the context. Each element of his harassment fits with the rhythm of the space in which it is perpetrated – the movement through tunnels, sitting stationary and 'watching' in the carriages where there are bystanders, and two verbal intrusions in spaces where a brief interaction would not be uncommon. His modus operandi of approaching Rach follows the ebb and flow of the network, and as such, conceals it from the view of other passengers.

Another form of sexual harassment that occurs on the Underground is what Brooks Gardner (1995) terms 'romanticized' sexual harassment. This more commonly plays out on late-night journeys, or on the 'night-Tube' (the Friday and Saturday service that runs through the night on five of the busiest lines). In the terranean night-time economy, social interactions are imbued with the crackle of excitement and possibility that comes from ambiguous and spontaneous connections, many of which are driven by continuous, heavy drinking (Smith, 2014). Leaching between the cracks of this 'transgressive ambiance' (Hobbs et al., 2005), sexual harassment is also rife in these spaces. As well as incidents of rape, assault and drink spiking, Gunby et al. (2020) theorise that, in this environment, the overarching forms of common unwanted sexual attention are 'the pick-up routine', and 'showing off for the lads'. Whilst separate from the clubs and bars above, at this time of night, being on the Underground does not signify the end of the night, but an extension of it, as animated carriages offer further opportunity for fleeting social connections. As Urry (2007) considers, trains and stations can be arenas of unanticipated social exchange. Thus, as blurry-eyed revellers retreat across the city in the early hours, the intoxicating atmospheres they have occupied become mobile, clinging to their skin like the smell of smoke, and spilling over in the space of the night-time Tube carriages, bringing with them the possibility of lax and playful social interaction. Though this kind of exchange can be a source of fleeting connection (Hubbard, 2012; Urry, 2007), in some circumstances it can creep from amicable to threatening. Rose tells of her experience on a late-night weekend train that was hosting a cacophony of drunk revellers travelling across the city. She reflects on how the ambiance of the network often shifts at this time of night to become a more extroverted space.

'There's a different vibe .... after a night out people are less embarrassed and less polite, there's license to do whatever they want to do ... maybe more pushy in their conversation'. She then describes an interaction with a man during her journey home: 'I was on the tube coming home, it must've been half 11 or something, it was late, and it was a Friday or a Saturday so there were lots of people a bit drunk or whatever. And I was wearing my red lipstick ... I'd just been out dancing. This guy came and sat next to me ... I think he was with some friends, and he came and sat and he started talking to me, and like I told you, I like to chat to people on the tube, I don't mind, so I engaged with the conversation that he started, it wasn't really a conversation just like uhhh hi you had a good night, yeaah you yaaah woo you alright ... he started getting closer and closer and uhm, like pushed himself right close to me. And my body language at that point, I was still being polite, but the thing is I had this problem where I didn't just want to be like, fuck off mate so I was still being polite to him but I was being really short with my answers ... and then his station came and before he got off he leaned across me and was like it's been so nice like talking to you ... and he tried to kiss me and at that point I put my hand on his face and pushed him away from my face ... eventually his friends were like come on mate, stop and pulled him off'. 'He wasn't being malicious, he was just overstepping the mark, an idiot, he was drunk ... he just thought he had the right to do that'.

Jules was on her way home from a late event on a Friday night when a man got on to the train and started talking to her: 'I got on the tube, it was quarter past 11, so it was late. And somebody got on the tube, he'd obviously been out partying and he came and sat next to me and started chatting. And to be honest, he got on at Tottenham court road and he looked like he'd just come from Soho and I assumed that he was gay. Then he started chatting and it became clear that actually he wanted sex .... And I said no, and he said well then why did you talk to me? And I'd misread his signals completely which happens to me very often. I don't think I was giving any off but there you go. Just being friendly, but because I'd spoken to him, he felt he was owed something more. Anyway, he then got quite grumpy and kept grabbing at me and so I stood up and went down to the other end of the tube and sat on a different chair, and he followed me. So at this point I was sitting down and he was standing over me and he kept leaning in to try and ... I'm not sure if he was trying to touch my face or kiss my face, but he kept doing that and coming towards my face. And I put my hands firmly in the middle of his chest pushing him away and saying no go away. And I must've done that 5 times, pushed him away and said go away'.

In a refraction of the activity in the night-time economy resounding in the city above, at these points in time the regulating norms of Simmel's (1903) 'blasé outlook' and Goffman's (1963) 'civil inattention' are diluted, as passengers become more open to spontaneous interactions with fellow travellers. We can discern from all the stories presented above how experiences of sexual harassment on the Underground are moulded by the various rhythms that flow through it depending on the time of day and activity in the city above. In Rose's and Jules' stories, we see how the overflowing of night-time economy sociabilities into the space of the Tube acts to alter the ambiance of the carriages. In this environment, the normalcy of fleeting and spontaneous interaction is exploited in order to engage women in ambiguous interactions that they are unable to easily withdraw from. Ruth's and Sheila's experiences offer examples of how, at peak rush hour times, the static crush of commuters means physical assault is perpetrated that is invisible to fellow passengers and experienced as confusing for the victim. In Grace's and Carla's stories from when they were younger, men masturbated in public space, in broad daylight, but in a way that was, again, unnoticed by other passengers. Furthermore, the trapped-ness of the carriage meant that the girls were forced to endure these visual assaults. In all of these stories, the rhythms and sociabilities of the space act to facilitate and conceal specific forms of sexual harassment, at particular times of day.

Etiquette

As we explored in the previous chapter, there are specific social rules, or 'Tube etiquette' that dominate the accepted and expected modes of behaviour within the London Underground. A concept that we have already touched upon throughout the book so far will now be given specific focus. Linking specifically to behaviour in public space, Erving Goffman's concept of 'civil inattention' refers to when individuals engage in a delicate balance between acknowledging the presence of others, whilst also respecting their privacy. Put simply, it refers to the right to be private in public. It is a highly useful concept to understand the nuance of often non-verbal, subtle public interactions. In condensed spatio-social environments such as public transport, it is not unusual to engage in brief, non-intrusive glances, offering others an awareness of their presence, without invading their personal (mental and physical) space. Clearly, the perpetration of sexual harassment abuses this norm, but, it also significantly structures how women react, in the moment, to these intrusions for fear of disturbing other passengers and being judged for doing so.

> Eliza describes two experiences of assault. The first took place on a busy weekend tube: 'It was quite busy, but I was so engrossed in this book, I wasn't really aware of who was around me. And I slowly began to be aware that something … there was a pressure on me. And it was only when I felt a pain that I kind of took notice and came out of my book. And I realised that there was this quite old guy. He was standing in front of me and he was pressing

his fist so hard, like against my vagina basically. But he must've done it so slowly that I didn't realise … in London you don't notice sometimes when your personal space is being invaded because you're so used to it. So, I didn't even notice that this guy had started pushing his fist, until it hurt, until it physically hurt me'.

Eliza considers how, in the moment she 'just wanted to push him away, shout at him'. However, she was worried that reacting overtly would disrupt the carriage: 'I didn't want to deal with the embarrassment or humiliation of people looking at me, judging me and probably not even helping'.

The second incident she talks about involves a man rubbing his erection against her. She describes her reaction: 'I turned round and really stared at the guy and moved away purposefully and dug my elbow and moved him away with my elbow. But again, I was too scared and embarrassed to make a fuss, that's the thing with me about keeping the peace on the tube and not wanting to cause a disruption that will make other people feel uncomfortable, or panic anyone. So that kind of keeping really silent and dealing with it in a different way'.

Her perception of the social nature of the Underground overrode her bodily desire to respond to both these incidents. She understood, that by blatantly reacting, she would break the barrier constructed by the collective enactment of civil inattention, leading to tension and embarrassment. Instead, she responds in a similar way to how her assault was perpetrated – corporeally, silently and unobserved by fellow passengers. Here, the rhythms and sociabilities of the carriage regulated both his action and her response. Eliza's desire not to draw attention to herself or make a scene was echoed by several other women who were forced to negotiate an experience of harassment or assault on a busy carriage.

After being groped on a busy tube, Emmy felt constrained in her response: 'And there's a lot of people around, because it was a packed carriage, so I guess I didn't want to make a scene, so I felt embarrassed, awkward …. It's really hard to break that silence … there's no eye contact … there's no talking, everyone's in their own world, trying to get through it because it's the part of the day that's a means to an end, trying to get to work. Nobody is present, they're just getting through it as quickly as possible'.

This speaks directly to Bissell's (2010) notion of rail carriages possessing 'affective atmospheres' which can lead passengers to semiconsciously adopt collective behaviours. We also see from the last couple of examples, how 'moral minimalism' rears its head within the space of the Tube and contributes significantly to these atmospheres. We see how women who 'know' the Tube, hold a strong belief that no one will support them if they react. When moral minimalism takes hold, social order is dominated by efforts to deny, minimise, contain and avoid conflict, and when conflict does arise with strangers, Baumgartner (1988) theorises that people 'do nothing and wait for the offender to move on or for the situation to resolve itself' (p. 105). This makes it harder for women being harassed to transgress these dominant socio-spatial norms, and their own internalisation of the social order of moral minimalism on the Tube. There is some existing research that draws attention to how women often do not react to sexual harassment in transport environments for fear of the situation escalating into violence (Horii & Burgess, 2012; Neupane & Chesney-Lind, 2013), but we see here that women do not just 'freeze' or keep silent due to an innate fear response (though for some women this does play a role). Rather, responses are regulated to synchronise with the social 'decorum' of the carriage and an internalisation and enactment of moral minimalism. Neglecting to recognise the pervasive impact of social norms is to disregard the nuances of spatio-temporal mobilities that interact with women's agency when they are forced to negotiate such experiences. Another element that comes forth in Emmy's account is that many of these negotiations are explicitly connected to the fact that these incidents of sexual harassment and the atmosphere of collective civil inattention in which they occur, are happening 'on the move'.

The peripatetic quality of the Tube carriage renders it what Augé (1995) defines as 'placeless', places that are characterised by profuse mobility. As Emmy considers, the only reason for being in the liminal space of public transport is to get somewhere else (Urry, 2007) and subsequently, travellers tend to want to minimise their journeying time. This connects with Goffman's idea of 'allocation involvement'. Conceptualised as part of his dramaturgical perspective on the social world, allocation involvement refers to how we strategically manage and distribute our attention in public social interactions in order to control our presentation of self. It is, in part, a process of engagement and disengagement. In transport environments, people can purposefully (dis)engage with those around them, as there is a shared focus on reaching the destination with as much predictability and as little disturbance as possible, thus, all other involvements are secondary and generally deemed worth avoiding. This has a significant impact on how women reacted to sexual harassment in the moment, with many of them not wanting to disrupt or elongate their journeys.

> When a man rubbed up against Charlie during an evening rush hour, she says how she 'wanted to get off the tube, but also I didn't because I wasn't where I wanted to be … I was entitled to be there and using it to get home, getting off would have slowed me down'.

> Earlier, we focussed on Carla's experience of a man masturbating at her on a quiet carriage. When this happened, she was on her way to meet a friend, and she spoke about how her reaction to this incident was mitigated by the fact that she was on the tube, on her way somewhere: 'Walking away wasn't an option, and I was already late, so I just kind of looked away and stayed on until my stop'.

Hearing these stories reminded me of my experience on the London bus, how I was disgusted and appalled by the man masturbating, but still didn't 'react' overtly. Except I did. I chose, like Charlie and Carla, to wait until my stop, get off the bus and carry on with my day. In some ways, like Gardner's (1995) observation that women manage power by not reacting to street harassment, these refusals to slow down are a resistance to the friction that is often imposed by men's intrusions. Overall, these stories collectively show how the space-specific rhythms, etiquette and sociabilities nudge against women's agency to morph and shape their immediate reactions to sexual harassment.

Brief Encounters

Here, I will reiterate the opening quote of the chapter from Urry (2007, p. 109), who describes train stations and carriages as '… places of unexpected social interchange as people's lives from distant parts are contingently brought together, often only for brief encounters: before the characters move away'. The very point of public transport is its transience, and its ephemeral nature plays a significant role in offering cover for deviant and criminal behaviour. As we have seen, for some women, particularly those who were assaulted during rush hours, the moment of intrusion was distorted with uncertainty. The confusion they felt around whether they were being purposefully victimised meant they were not able to process or respond to the incident in a way that they felt was appropriate to the situation and congruent to their sense of self.

> Tia reflects on how her reaction to being groped was shaped by the ambiguity of the situation: 'The thing itself now doesn't bother me so much, I'm not like traumatised or anything. But the weird thing, the thing that I think I still think about sometimes and what sticks in my head, is that I didn't really do anything. I sort of just let it happen. I actually just let this man put his hand between my legs and didn't kick off. But I think also like, it took some time to actually realise. I don't know if it was shock or just sort of, what, is this actually happening here? Could it be something else or … I don't even know but I think I was just confused more than anything and I missed my window to call him out. That still gets to me'.

She recognises the significance of temporality and transience here, as she discusses the appropriate 'window' in which she feels able to react (in the next chapter, we see Kath use the same language to describe her own reaction). In this instance, she misses what she perceives to be the right time to speak due to her uncertainty around the man's intent and whether what she could feel was *really* happening.

> Demi talks about a similar experience when she was in London for a business trip and travelling just after morning rush hour: 'It

wasn't massively busy, but enough people that when you bumped together you didn't think anything of it. So when I felt someone bump against me, to start with I didn't think anything of it, but then right in my ear there was heavy breathing and I was thinking that's a bit weird you're standing a bit near. And then I felt him bumping into me repeatedly and I could feel his erection. So I thought this isn't ok. But because I was in shock for a few seconds I didn't do anything, like is this actually happening to me right now … a guy is basically grinding into your back whilst heavy breathing in your ear, this is grim. When it first happened, when he first started rubbing himself against me I didn't really realise what was happening. There are a lot of people on there and he did it in time with the swaying of the tube carriage …. By the time I really realised, like properly, what was going on, that he was actually rubbing against me, it was too late because it was my stop'.

Again, these experiences challenge the notion that women do not react overtly simply because of fear (Pain, 1991). We can link this back to Koskela's (1997) work on 'bold breakings' where she argues that, in response to street harassment, women often experience a sense of boldness and fear at the same time. These stories show that, amidst the mobile and rhythmic space of the Underground, women must also contend with feelings of uncertainty and confusion that mould their experiences and responses. This is an important contribution to work that has argued we must circumvent reductive portrayals of women as submissive and vulnerable, and rather do justice to the complexity of women's feelings and (internal) negations that constitute the foundations for their visible reactions.

Finally, it is important to address how the ephemerality of the transport environment gave women the impression that their situation was fleeting and temporary. This implicated their decisions around whether it was worthwhile confronting their harasser (and dealing with possible escalation, 'getting it wrong', and the potential shame and embarrassment caused by the disdain from other travellers), considering that the situation was temporary, and the journey would soon be over.

> Chloe described her decision to stay where she was whilst a man rubbed against her from behind, in the hope that the interaction would not be prolonged: 'I thought just hang in there and wait for the next stop, then he might leave … but stop after stop he didn't'.

Shuttling through tunnels between stations, the Tube carriage is recurrently sequestered from the world above (the sensation of being 'cut off' is exacerbated by the lack of phone or Wi-Fi signal on most lines). This sense of disconnectedness meant Chloe felt trapped and unable to remove herself from the situation. Yet the arrival at each station offered a glimmer of hope that the offender would leave without her having to confront him. This is an illustration of the uncomfortableness or sense of arrhythmia that arises when conflicting rhythms meet – in this instance, the body is *stationary* whilst being *transported* at a pace uncontrolled by the individual. This is yet another nexus of multiple rhythms that implicates women's reactions to sexual harassment within this dynamic space.

> We see this play out in Talia's encounter: 'I think I'd been at a work event and I'd had a few drinks but I wasn't drunk, I was like in that mode, cos I'm quite chatty anyway, where I'm quite happy to sort of like chat to people …. He was sitting next to me and he just pulled my hand on to his lap … he wasn't doing anything dodgy, he just held it. But I froze. I completely froze …. And other people were getting on and off the tube and it was like a really quiet tube, only 4 or 5 people in our carriage and I desperately wanted to say to somebody can you get this guy off me, but I couldn't look at him or speak to him, to say can you get off me … I was completely frozen, it was a really odd situation and it lasted all the way home, we must be talking about 15 minutes, and the longer that it went on for the longer that I felt like I couldn't, and I kept trying to like subtly move it … I was genuinely frightened you know …. If I do something to him is he gonna like kick off. And I kept thinking you know when we were at stops to say something but then like you know there's the hustle and bustle of everyone getting off like do I say something or do I get off. Now looking back on it I think I should've just got off, even though that's him taking me out of my space but I think at the same time I just wanted to get home, I still don't understand it, I've looked back at the situation …, my mind was going ten to the dozen, and I just kept thinking you know, this is such odd behaviour but what's he going to do next if I escalate it. But I think why it bothers me so much is that it was so, it wasn't violent, it wasn't that he was trying to touch me in a gross way, or anything like that, it almost wasn't sexual. And I feel like that was more about power, I feel like he knew what he was doing and it was about controlling me in someway'.

Talia articulates fear of escalation as a central part of her emotional response, and how this acts in conjunction with the mobile, confined nature of the space. If she had made the decision to get off the Tube, she would have significantly disrupted her journey. If she reacted overtly, she would then have to deal with his response (which she feared) in a confined environment. Each time the train passed through a station, she (re)negotiated her decision, until she arrived at her stop. The more time that passed, the less she felt able to respond. In a similar situation, Layla described how, when a man was pushing his erection up against her on a busy Tube, she considered trying to leave at every station by merging with the fluctuation of people getting on and off the carriage: 'I kept thinking, well only three, two, one more stops to go'. Again, if we reflect back to Grace's experience as a 14-year-old when a man masturbated at her on an empty carriage, she remembers thinking about how long she would have to endure it for '… one stop to go. How long can that take? Well apparently, it takes a really long time!' Here, we see the subjective nature of temporalities play out. Whilst, as Urry (2007) considers, high speed travel tends to compress time, the personal experience of this can be mitigated by a disruption to psychological rhythms that causes time to stretch and drag. Here, incidents of abnormal behaviour in the form of sexual harassment cause the sensation of temporal friction and slowing down, overruling the (bodily experience of) mechanical, fast pace of the Tube.

The perpetrators of these offences also exploit the transient nature of the space. A number of women had experiences where the man who harassed them used the movement of the trains and crowds to 'slip away'.

> After being groped on a rush hour carriage, Ruth said: 'Then the doors opened and everyone got off … the guy got off … everyone carries on with their journey … the tube, it's such an ephemeral thing, you're not there for long, you just get through it like oh it'll be over in a minute …. And then you think, the moment's passed, there's nothing I can do about it'.

> Eliza similarly discussed how after groping her on a rush hour tube the man 'slunk away down the carriage … he got off and then disappeared into the mass of people'.

Here, the incessant movement of both trains and people allows the perpetrator to slink away and dissolve anonymously into the maze of the Underground. In this final section of the chapter, 'Brief Encounters', we have discerned how the mobile features of a transport network act to significantly mould experiences of sexual harassment. The temporary nature of the interaction between the victim and the offender often led to women not having time to fully comprehend and process the intrusion before the situation came to an end. As well as this, the expectation that the situation would soon resolve itself (by the journey ending) impacted their decisions to not respond overtly. Paying attention to the mobile landscape of transport spaces and the subjective interpretations and experiences of time within them, offers a deeper understanding as to why many women do not confront offenders in these environments.

Using a mobilities approach, this chapter has sought to discern some key features of incidents of sexual harassment on the London Underground. Three key conceptual observations have been outlined as significant in how sexual harassment is perpetrated and experienced on the Underground, these being: how the rhythms of the city and the Underground facilitate and conceal harassment; women's fear of disrupting the social etiquette of the space; and women's perceptions of the situations as brief and temporary encounters. This chapter has shown that the way in which sexual harassment is happening in a transport environment is distinct from the way it is perpetrated on the streets and in workplace settings. Whilst there are similarities to street harassment, its unique spatial, temporal and social nature means that sexual harassment that occurs in transit is perpetrated and experienced in a specific way, facilitated and constricted by the environment.

The characteristic traits of the Underground are truly temporal and rhythmic, and the women's stories shared here illustrate the real, social impact of these rhythms, and how within this rhythmic ensemble, women negotiate the disruptions caused by this form of gendered violence.

Chapter 6

'After': The Impact of Sexual Harassment – Remembering and Resisting Across Time and Space

Abstract

This chapter focusses on what happens 'after' an incident of sexual harassment. It explores the impact that the memory of sexual harassment has on women and their mobilities in the city over time. By employing 'memory' as a sociological concept in order to link space, time and women's embodied experiences, this chapter aims to understand the negotiations that women undertake in order to 'deal with' the incidents of sexual harassment and claim back their mobility and freedom. It will pay attention to how the impact is not static, but rather shifts and morphs over time and space. Importantly, this analysis moves beyond simply discussing women's fear and vulnerability and makes room for a consideration of how sexual harassment on public transport is negotiated and resisted, and how the experiences or memories are also suppressed and can, at times, act to embolden women in their urban mobilities. Using the conceptual framework structured around mobilities, space and time this chapter offers a unique analysis of the impact of sexual harassment in a transport environment.

Keywords: Sexual harassment; London Underground; public transport; urban mobility; memory

Mind the Gender Gap: A Mobilities Perspective of Sexual Harassment on the
London Underground, 95–111

doi:10.1108/978-1-83753-026-720241006

It's like a process you go through ... I started off feeling violated, and then I felt shocked at the same time and upset and I went on to feeling angry, like how dare someone do that to me, I was just minding my own business on a tube train. Then you feel determined that you want to do something, then when you've finally done that, gone to the police or done something else that makes you feel better, then you start to accept what happened. (Sheila)

You're damned whatever you do ... the 'right' way to act, it's never fixed either and you're constantly negotiating for your space and renegotiating for your righteousness. (Kath)

As an adult looking back on it, I'm like mate, you did not need to feel guilty or ashamed, tell your Mum. But I know I would never have in that situation. If that happened to me now, I'd be much more like, what's your problem get away from me ... it wouldn't frighten me as much, that kind of thing, but yeah we get used to it .... (Ellie)

Ever since, if a man's ... like I remember there was this guy, and he was very tall and his hand brushed my bum and I said listen I'm really sorry but this has happened to me ... and for the rest of the journey he had his hands up like it's fine .... (Becky)

I still feel pretty safe on the tube. But I walk through that tunnel pretty much every time I commute, and pretty much every time I sort of see him in my head, you know. (Rachel)

In this chapter, we explore the impact that sexual harassment in a transport environment has on women's negotiations of urban space and on their mobilities in the city over time. We will consider the immediate impact of these intrusions, and how women 'deal with' these encounters in the moments that directly follow. We will also pay attention to how the spectre of these experiences exists in women's periphery, shifting in form and focus over time and space, contorting women's mobilities in the city. There is existing work that offers important insights into both the short- and long-term impact of sexual harassment, and this will briefly be reviewed. Then, to contribute a new angle to these discussions, I introduce *memory* as a useful sociological concept, reasoning that it allows us to link space, time, and women's embodied experience. In doing so, this reveals that the impact of sexual harassment is not static or contained, but a mobile, malleable process that is regularly reconstructed depending on the contours of time and space.

We explore this phenomenon through the stories of Kath, Ellie, Beth and Rachel, tracing the negotiations that these four women undertake in order to manage the immediate experience and memory of sexual harassment and claim back their mobility. Kath talks about how she was assaulted twice by the same person only weeks apart, and how the first incident emboldened her reaction to the second. Ellie reflects on a childhood incident, considering how her understanding of what happened has changed over the years, and how the memory of the incident has impacted on her mobilities over time. Beth, who was groped by a businessman on a rush hour Tube talks about the process of reporting to the police, and how moving through the criminal justice system stipulated the process of remembering. Rachel was assaulted in an Underground tunnel and talks about how past experiences of sexual violence impacted on her reaction here. Understanding these stories through the approach outlined above, we move beyond sanitising and reducing women's complex responses to narrate a fixed state of fear and vulnerability. It allows us to see how sexual harassment in public space is negotiated and resisted, and how, alongside fear, these experiences and their memories are purposefully suppressed or brought into focus in order to reclaim space and mobility.

The Impact of Sexual Harassment in Public Space

When considering the immediate impact of sexual violence, research often focusses on how it leads to increased levels of fear (Keane, 1995; Pain, 1991; Stanko, 1993). This immediate fear is experienced in an intensely sensorial and corporeal way. Brooks Gardner (1995, p. 211) describes how reactions to public harassment are often physical, giving examples of flinching, muscle tension, and internal – stopping breathing, feeling numb, feeling like jelly. Lefebvre (2004, p. 31) writes how the body can experience a disruption of rhythms or *arrhythmia* and describes this as: 'in suffering, in confusion, a particular rhythm surges up and imposes itself: palpitation, breathlessness, pains in the place of satiety'. These descriptions can be understood as interoceptive sensory responses to fear (Holt & Lewis, 2024), and they are necessary and useful to recognise the immediate, fear-based physical reaction to sexual harassment, as it often plays a key role in dictating the visible external response to harassment, such as freezing (though, as we explored in the previous chapter these responses are also implicated by the social space in which they occur).

Yet it is important to acknowledge that this is not the *only* or *normal* response to such an intrusion, rather, just one on a wide spectrum of multifarious possible reactions. As Lefebvre (2004) considers, we become more acutely aware of our rhythms when they suffer some irregularity – when in a state of arrythmia, they are given more attention. As such, those women who *do not* have fear responses, whose internal rhythms are *less* disturbed or disrupted, may find it difficult to articulate or make this (lack of) sensation tangible and known. These experiences can then be side-lined and neglected from analysis, mitigating the social and academic understanding of these reactions. As Koskela (2010, p. 305) considers 'It is so frequently said that women are afraid that it seems almost indecent to say that they are not'. She considers how women's fear is often regarded as normal, whilst boldness and defiance are considered to be risky and subversive. Indeed, much existing literature omits how women's immediate responses to sexual harassment are often positioned between the binaries of confrontation and passivity. Similarly, when considering the immediate *external* response to sexual harassment, it is important to conceptualise 'doing nothing' or 'not reacting' as active choices, rather than framing them as passivity. Brooks Gardner (1995) describes how women she spoke to in her research on street harassment felt they were managing power by pretending nothing was happening. Vera-Gray and Kelly (2020) consider how 'not reacting' can be a form of embodied safety work, and Madriz (1997) states how women ignore or deny their fear to minimise the harmful impact it could have. Furthermore, Sandberg and Ronnblom (2013) recognise how women in their research expressed ambivalence towards their own fear and argued that this attitude can be framed as an expression of resistance.

Similar themes exist in the literature that focusses on the long term impact of sexual harassment. Much of this work has emphasised how these intrusions cause an increased sense of vulnerability, leading to heightened levels of fear of similar experiences happening again (Mellgren et al., 2018). Painter (1992) and Valentine (1990) argue that experiences of sexual harassment can bolster fear of public spaces and cause women to perceive (male) strangers as unpredictable, leading to women adopting strategies to avoid further victimisation in public space (Keane, 1998). These strategies or behavioural modifications are what Vera-Gray and Kelly (2020) term 'safety work' and are consequential as they can act to decrease women's freedoms and quality of public life (Pain, 1991; Vera-Gray, 2018). This has also been explicitly connected to mobilities. Keane (1998) frames this fear and its adaptations as a 'mobility restrictor', and Ceccato (2017) and Loukaitou-Sideris (2014) articulate the impact of fear of sexual harassment on transport as impairing mobility. However, it is also important to recognise that additional fear is not the only active ingredient in long-term negotiations of experiences of sexual harassment. Pain (1997, p. 238) highlights how, because women are acutely aware of the constraints imposed upon them by (fear of) violence, they are also angry about it, and are 'ingenious in their efforts to limit the effect of these constraints'. Koskela (2010, p. 309) recognises how women who are harassed in a space they use regularly often do not then perceive the space as dangerous due to its familiarity, and how 'making use of space a part of one's daily routine erases the myth of danger from it'. This signifies that even those who experience fear often take active measures to (re)negotiate their right to the city. This work is useful in understanding normative perceptions of the impact of sexual harassment in the short and long term. However, I contend that by using the concept of memory in tandem with rhythmanalysis, we can understand how memories of sexual harassment ebb and flow in form and prominence, offering us a nuanced analysis of how women negotiate and manage the impact of sexual harassment in transit over time and space, thus framing 'impact' as something capricious and unfixed.

The Rhythms of Remembering

The concept of memory relates to the way in which we reconceptualise the past in relation to the present and future. A sociology of memory (in comparison to psychoanalytic and cognitive psychological approaches) examines the way in which individual and collective memories are formed and transformed over time within social and cultural frameworks (Halbwachs, 1950; Oakley, 2016). In one of the earliest studies of memory by a sociologist, Jane Addams (1916, 2002) frames personal recollection as an ongoing individual, subjective, emotional, cognitive and social process. Keightley (2010, p. 56) frames remembering as '… a process of making sense of experience, of constructing and navigating complex temporal narratives and structures and ascribing meaning not only to the past, but to the present and future also'. It is memory that makes the past a lived process that is reconceptualised and negotiated in everyday experience. In this chapter, the temporal nature of memory helps to discern how incidents of sexual harassment are (re)remembered and (re)negotiated over time and how their impact on women's experiences of mobility in urban space is ever-changing. So, we see how a focus on memory encourages us to observe the entangling of past and present in order to make sense of both. In simple terms, we use the *past* to make sense of the *present*, and simultaneously, we use the *present* to make sense of the *past*.

Emotional and Mobile Memories

The 'remembering' of incidents of sexual violence has been theorised, and understood in practice, as a form of 'traumatic memory'. Trauma is said to escape full consciousness (Caruth, 1995) and therefore, these kinds of memories are often fragmented and incoherent (Sotgiu & Galati, 2007). Indeed, Hardy et al. (2009) have considered how memories of rape and sexual assault are contingent on this impaired processing of memory. It has been widely recognised that trauma has continuing repercussions, impacting on a person's ability to perceive and navigate life after the event(s). It is possible that some women in this research may consider their experiences as traumatic (though this language was not explicitly used). However, a more appropriate term for how many of the women conceptualised and reflected on their experiences, is an 'emotional memory'. Tromp et al. (1995) describe how emotional memories with intense affect are remembered more accurately and are more accessible than neutral events. The stories recalled below, are perhaps better framed, as Pickering and Keightley (2009) theorise, as painful or emotional memories, rather than trauma, as they have been integrated into women's lives and they were able to recall them in detail (such detail which, in fact, took many participants by surprise). Therefore, it is arguably more appropriate, in this instance, to frame incidents of sexual harassment as 'emotionally intense events'.

Another significant aspect of traumatic or emotional memories that is particularly related to sexual violence, is how these experiences are redefined and acknowledged over time. Even when, by legal definition, incidents meet the criteria for rape or sexual assault, women often do not label their experiences as such (Bondurant, 2001; Fisher et al., 2003). This has been written about extensively with regard to unacknowledged rape, particularly when perpetrated by an intimate partner (Jaffe et al., 2017; Kahn et al., 2003). Some literature frames this 'denial' as avoidance, or as a coping mechanism to deal with a traumatic encounter (Roth & Newman, 1991), and others consider how the normalisation of harmful and criminal behaviours impacts the way victims understand what has happened (Hlavka, 2014; Sinko et al., 2021). Due to the initial disengagement with experiences, the labelling of incidents is often delayed (Cleere & Lynn, 2013). Redefinition over time can be caused by numerous factors including a shift in societal attitudes and the individual's life trajectory. Botta and Pingree (1997) also highlight how the sharing of common stories is an important way in which women recognise and redefine their experiences as assault or rape (this resonates with the outpouring of stories as a consequence of the #MeToo movement). As explored below, memories of sexual harassment are reconceptualised and redefined over time, as women traverse personal and social landscapes that shift their understanding of their own experience. In turn, this continual reconceptualisation impacts how the experience, in tandem with other encounters, continues to play a fluctuating role in their negotiations of urban space.

Benjamin (1968) writes how memory and the metropolis are interwoven as memory shapes, and is in turn, shaped by the urban setting. We can link this to women's experiences and memories of sexual harassment and how they interplay with the city spaces. Warr (1984) speaks of women's propensity to transfer past experiences and memories of victimisation to present situations. This links to women being increasingly fearful in public space after experiencing sexual intrusion (Koskela, 2010; Loukaitou-Sideris & Fink, 2009). 'Mental mapping' is a term lodged within urban studies, geography and social psychology (Lynch, 1975; Tuan, 1975) that regards remembering, knowing and negotiating restrictions in the urban environment (Middleton, 2009). A person's mental map emerges out of their physical, emotional and sensorial engagement with the space (Ingold, 2007), and these maps are understood as mobile and unstable. For women who have experienced sexual harassment in public space, these encounters are subsumed into their (subjective) understandings of what is safe and what is risky. As we see in the stories below, the intrusions distort notions of predictability in familiar spaces, and render the sense of ownership and freedom in the city as precarious and something that must be renegotiated. By conceptualising memories as not only temporal but also spatial, we can see how they must be understood as mobile to allow us to grasp the viscosity of their impact on women as they move through urban space.

Negotiating the Memory and Impact of Sexual Harassment

We will now follow Kath, Ellie, Beth and Rachel's stories to illustrate how, following an experience of sexual harassment on the London Underground, women negotiated the impact of the incident over time and space. Conceptualising these memories as spatio-temporally implicated shows that their meanings are not fixed and can be redefined over time. It allows recognition of how sexual harassment has disrupted women's freedom, and also how they have actively resisted and minimised disruption. It highlights that amidst confusion and fear, women also have active agency in their negotiation of public space after experiencing sexual harassment.

Kath

As a 40-year-old, born and bred Londoner, Kath has travelled on the Underground for as long as she can remember and describes having a 'misguided sense of invincibility' when confidently navigating the network. Yet she reflects on how two experiences of sexual harassment that were committed by the same man, a few weeks apart, disrupted her notion of freedom in the city that she knows and loves. Travelling in the early evening, Kath recalls her internal thought process and physical reaction to a man putting his hands between her legs, and then over her body:

> I'm like, I'm reasonably sure I'm being assaulted .... Then a couple of stops on I'm like yeah I'm definitely being assaulted and now I haven't done anything about it, I've not moved, I'm frozen and he's had his knuckles between my legs for a few tube stops ....

Her experience is initially dominated by uncertainty. As Gardner (1995, p. 154) states 'caught between a number of possible lines of action, a woman can be frozen into inaction'. Whilst freezing appears to be an intense corporeal, physical reaction, it is also what Koskela (2010, p. 306) describes as 'reasoning'. Not moving is an embodied reaction implicated by social, spatial, temporal complexity, and its occurrence reveals an active tension, or friction between rhythms. Lefebvre (2004, p. 47) also recognises that although freezing may seem instinctive and natural 'the representation of the natural falsifies situations. Something passes as natural precisely when it conforms perfectly and without apparent effort to accepted models, to the habits valorised by a tradition ...'. Freezing and 'inaction' are commonly attributed as embodied responses to fear, yet Kath's elaboration shows that surprise and uncertainty are, in her case, more significant:

> You sort of second-guess yourself don't you, which I think is a significant thing about the tube ... because you've got that window. Is that? Maybe they're not doing it deliberately, I don't want to make a fuss ... you don't want to be oversensitive and accuse someone when they're going about their business .... I have to make a conscious, active choice. The opposite of submissive, I have to make an active decision, and to do that I have to be sure of what's happened and I have to make that choice quickly, in that window, before it becomes really awkward. Second-guessing, maybe he doesn't like the draft near the door ... all this shit going on in my head .... It's that fatal period of: is it? By the time you've worked it out, you've missed your window to make fuss.

Lefebvre (2004, p. 52) says about how irregular rhythms produce antagonistic effects 'it throws out of order and disrupts; it is symptomatic of a disruption ...'. Due to the surprise and uncertainty that Kath experienced, this 'freezing' prevents her from acting overtly. She also highlights how the transitory nature impacted on her reaction: 'it's nonsense but I have explicitly thought this in my head … oh well, it's only three stops to Baker Street, how much worse can it get?'. This highlights the significance of the spatial and temporal complexity of negotiating such an experience on the Tube. Kath also discusses how this particular reaction unsettled her due to it being incongruent with her sense of self:

> It bothers me, I consider myself to be a strong feminist, I'm known for having a big mouth and an attitude. I'm known for being a bolshie bird, and I consider myself to be one, because I wouldn't take that kind of crap elsewhere, yet … again it happens.

This mirrors Gardner's (1995, p. 12) work in which she states 'women with highly developed politicised feminist consciousness were not always satisfied with their methods of handling harassment'. Memories form our identity (McQuire, 1998) as we construct coherent selves that have consistency over time. This formation of self takes place in everyday, individual experiences. As Wilson et al. (2009) consider, it involves the memory of the past self, an awareness of the present self and the anticipation of the future self, and Adam (1991, p. 71) posits that living beings are, from the depth of their temporal being, practising centres of action rather than perpetrators of fixed behaviour. This is supported by Kath's account of her subsequent experience. She describes how a few weeks later, the same man gets on at the same stop (Kilburn), which Kath describes as 'her station', and positions himself directly behind her on the Tube, and puts his hands on her again. She remembers thinking: 'I thought if I let this go, I'm going to live in fear of him'. This highlights that her '(re)action' is not immediate or instinctive but a deliberate response impacted by her previous experience:

> I turned around and I went get the fuck away from me. I said you've done this to me before, your hands are all over me and I'm not having you do this to me on my journey to work, I'm not living in fear of you, I'm not having it and he was like you crazy woman what are you talking about? And I said if that's the case you'll have no problem moving away from me then do you, so move.

Adam (1991, p. 147) purports that 'we are shown to relive the past and to learn from it; to use it for future action'. For Kath, the memory of the first incident impacts directly on her reaction to the second. She also discusses the tension she felt in negotiating her reactions saying: 'I end up feeling guilty because I've caused a fuss'. This draws attention to the importance of not having an established hierarchy of responses, and of not considering 'speaking out' or being active' as the most preferable way to react. Kath acknowledges this saying: 'You're damned whatever you do … the 'right' way to act, it's never fixed either and you're constantly negotiating for your space and renegotiating for your righteousness'.

She says 'It makes it sound like you've failed if you don't shout about it', but she also considers the difficulties that come with reacting overtly:

> Every time you laugh it off, every time your mates find it funny, it looks like you're not an ideal victim because you didn't say no. But you're also in a catch 22 because by taking control of that you're acting in a way that people aren't supposed to behave, you're being loud and out of place .... And it's that constant battle to stake your claim, mark out your own territory .... And it is so much about space and how you're able to stake out your territory, how much you compromise, you have in your head the idea that you've failed to conform to what a righteous victim does'.

Kath says she found it: 'challenging to my idea that I was free, to go about my business as I please ... they've taken your space away and that's definitely a lot of it and why you might feel so violated or uncomfortable'. As well as causing her to question her sense of self, it also affected her sense of urban competency and ownership of the city. However, the comparison between her two experiences shows how her initial reaction to the first incident was freezing out of surprise and uncertainty; she processed this reaction, and in the subsequent incident she is therefore more prepared and confronts her harasser, despite this causing her anxiety and internal friction.

Ellie

Ellie is 30 now and living in Brighton. She recalls her 12th birthday when she was visiting London with her Mum. Excited to be in the city and feeling grown up in her new, tight, sparkly dress, she wanted to feel independent, so she sat away from her Mum on the Tube. Over the course of the journey, she remembers being stared at intently by a man sitting opposite her, who, as she got up to leave, put his hand up her dress and tried to follow her. She discusses her immediate reaction to what happened:

> There was a whole load of stuff going on about how I felt about that at the time ... I felt ashamed, I didn't want to make a scene and I certainly didn't want to ask for my Mum either ... I was 12, I was grown up ... but yeah certainly an element of, I don't want anyone to see this is happening, so I'm just going to act normal ....'

The space is significant here, as is Lefebvre's (2004) notion of 'dressage' and the concealment of inner rhythms. Ellie, whilst experiencing a state of disruption and arrhythmia, forces herself to act in line with the social etiquette of the space. For her, her immediate reaction at the time was fear and self-blame, as she focussed instantly on her own appearance: 'I was so ... scared but also immediately ashamed of what I was wearing and conscious, and wishing I'd dressed down and wished I'd never bought that stupid dress and it was horrible'. Historically women and girls have been advised to manipulate their dress and behaviour for the sake of remaining safe and preventing crime (Gardner, 1990). Pain (1997) also considers how constantly reinforced notions about how women should be and present themselves in public space can lead to embodied knowledge that includes the inclination to internalise and engage in self-blame. Being 12 years old, for Ellie, this moment took on particular significance: 'It's the first time I can remember in my life, being looked at like that. And I knew that he wasn't just being starey, he was looking at me in a predatory, frightening way'. As a 'first', the moment becomes a meaningful and emotional memory that impacted her subsequently:

> I just felt it was the first time I was more aware of myself ... because I absolutely placed all the blame on me. I didn't blame him ... it was my fault because I was wearing that dress and so no, it didn't make me frightened of men, I just learnt to never dress like that again .... It impacted me for ages afterwards ... just feeling very ashamed, is the only way I can describe it. I just felt really ashamed, I never ... well I mean I wear tight clothes now, but for a long time afterwards I would never have worn anything like that again, like got my legs out ....

The immediate feeling of shame became a prolonged and embodied memory that permeated into the broader context of her life. As well as implicating her *presentation* of self (Goffman, 1955), it also had an effect on her *sense* of self: 'I still feel that really strongly when I look back, that's the first time anyone looked at me like that ... I never thought about myself in that way, never ever, it was the first time ever'. This links to work that has considered how our own bodies are brought into consciousness when we experience pain or discomfort (Cregan, 2006; Leder, 1990) or, a state of arrhythmia. For Ellie, the awareness that she is being sexualised disrupts her sense of self, making her acutely aware of her body and what she is wearing. Drawing attention to temporality, she also discusses the time it took to speak about the incident:

> I was so ashamed. I didn't talk to anyone about it at all, until a few years ago when I told my Mum ... yeah, years later, about 5 years ago I brought it up to my Mum, I was like, it was so horrible Mum ... I have lived with this, it was really scary.

This relates to what Pickering and Keightley (2009, p. 238) consider with regard to traumatic memories, where traumatic experience and the consequent repressed memory mean it is difficult to 'make storyable'. This shows the significance of temporality as to how such an experience is negotiated. The passing of time (13 years in this case) allowed feelings of shame to dissipate enough to share the experience. Furthermore, the phrase 'I have lived with this' shows how this memory has become imbedded into her 'autobiographical memory' (Misztal, 2003, p. 78) as something that she has been required to negotiate across time and space. Ellie reflects on how her judgement of the incident has altered over time:

> As an adult looking back on it, I'm like mate, you did not need to feel guilty or ashamed, tell your Mum. But I know I would never have in that situation. If that happened to me now, I'd be much more like, what's your problem get away from me ... it wouldn't frighten me as much, that kind of thing, but yeah we get used to it ....

She recognises that now she would act differently, yet also, as Adam (1991, p. 143) states, how '... the contemporary reliving is always inclusive of the inter-vening years, that these years are fundamentally implicated and resonate through the experience. The relived experience is different because of it'. This also links with literature that discusses how traumatic or emotional memories of sexual assault are redefined over time, allowing victims to redirect blame towards the perpetrator (Bondurant, 2001; Cleere & Lynn, 2013).

The spatial-temporal dimension is also significant in Ellie's account. She describes how it impacted her perception of the space of the Underground, say-ing: 'It totally made me petrified of the tube. And I suppose the thing about that as well was that I wasn't regularly using the tube'. Volkan (2002, p. 45) considers how people establish connections between past trauma and present or future threats. As a non-frequent traveller on the Tube, there is no familiarity or logic to it being relatively safe, therefore this incident became a formative memory, intrinsically associated with the space and increased her level of fear of the Underground. Ellie recognises this saying how as time has gone on she is less fearful of the space, in part due to this familiarity: 'my memories of it as a child are definitely ... always something horrible ... as an adult I don't notice that nearly as much, and I guess I've kind of got used to it'. This signifies the intersection of space, time and memory with regard to the lasting impact of sexual harassment. She also indicates how the incident has permeated her views of the Tube as an adult:

> I'm sure that incident has to do with how I feel about the tube now, in that it's not ... I wouldn't choose to go on the tube everyday if I can avoid it. I'm fairly, well very cautious about travelling alone because I've had a number of things happen to me ... sometimes I might have to get a tube back on my own ... but in that situation I don't feel safe.

Fear of a particular place can lead to avoidance or constrained behaviour (Ferraro, 1996), which can become a 'routine activity' (Keane, 1998, p. 63). Also noting 'avoidance' as significant in women's patterns of mobility, Gardner (1995, p. 202) describes how women have their own 'personal geography of public space', or, as mentioned earlier, possess a subjective 'mental map' of where is safe and where is dangerous. Reflecting on the incident 13 years later, it is clear that the memory of that childhood experience has impacted on Ellie's feeling of freedom and safety when she uses the Underground.

Becky

Becky is 31 years old, living in London and working in Canary Wharf. She describes an incident that happened around three years ago. On her way to work on a busy Tube, a man grabs her backside with both hands. She describes her immediate reaction saying: 'I turned around and I went, what are you doing? I nearly took a photo of him, but I wasn't feeling that brave .... And as soon as I challenged him, he said oh, I'm so sorry'. Here, the image of the passive commuter body situated within an anonymous and transitory space is exploited by the perpetrator. There is an assumption that women will not speak out, and that if they do the anonymity of the environment will act as a cover (as discussed in Chapter 5). Yet despite this, Becky reacted in an overt way, confronting her harasser. Yet she also hints at how her desired reaction was restricted by fear. This links to Koskela's (2010) claim that feelings of fear and boldness are rarely either/ or. It is important to recognise that women talking about their boldness, does not deny their fear. Following this initial reaction, Becky arrives at her stop and immediately goes to report the incident:

> I got off the tube and I went to the guys on the platform and said that guy's just assaulted me. And he left the building. They were the loveliest people. They took me up to the control room and put me on the phone to BTP ... and at that point I was actually fine, I just wanted to report it because it's important to report these things.

The fact that it was her regular journey (Northern Line to Bank and then DLR to Canary Wharf-South Quay) and she knew (by sight) the staff at the station, allowed her a sense of familiarity and reassurance: 'you feel ... it's kind of like a community because you go through the same stations every day. And the station staff rarely change and you kind of get used to it'. The cumulative knowledge of the space as safe and repetitive (Edensor, 2010; Lefebvre, 2004) gave her the confidence and encouragement to speak out immediately. After reporting, Becky went to work, and then to running practice. She describes how on the way home she felt a 'delayed reaction' of 'feeling his hands pressed against my bum'.

> And I remember I took a picture of myself on the tube, which I think I still have ... on the way home from training. I was like this is what it looks like to feel like this .... And I never posted this picture anywhere, I just took the picture on my phone and was like this is what I look like when I've been violated.

McQuire (1998) discusses how photography is used as a form of remembering and preservation. Becky's own negotiation of the experience was to make it more permanent and solidify the memory and how it felt. She monumentalises this moment and makes it significant in order to validate her own experience. Whilst her negotiation and ownership of the experience led her to feel empowered, she recognises how the process of reporting and going to court can be drawn out and time consuming, creating a friction between the desire to 'move on' and the desire for 'justice':

> The thing about not going to court, I can totally understand because it's an arduous process, spending 18 months waiting and then having to tell a police officer every time you book a holiday, and waiting and being told you need to keep this week free … I think I had moments where I was like I don't like this. And moments in the process of going to court … emotionally it kind of did get to me but I wasn't really aware of that when it was happening.

The process of going to court meant that the incident was still an everyday part of her life to be negotiated. As McQuire (1998, p. 164) states: 'Distance from the past is less than a simple measure of chronology'. In the long run, Becky considers how this incident has emboldened her claim to space. Crime prevention research has described how women who have been victims of crime subsequently adopt behaviours to avoid being victimised again (Ball & Wesson, 2017; Gekoski et al., 2015) and the impact that this has on mobility and therefore quality of life is also well documented (d'Arbois de Jubainville & Vanier, 2017; Loukaitou-Sideris et al., 2014). Yet as Koskela (2010, p. 205) states 'Women are not merely objects in space where they experience restrictions and obligations; they also actively produce, define and reclaim space'. Becky described how the incident caused her to moderate her behaviour on the Tube:

> Ever since, if a man's … like I remember there was this guy, and he was very tall and his hand brushed my bum and I said listen I'm really sorry but this has happened to me, and I told him what happened to me and I just get a little bit freaked out, would you mind raising your hands. And he said that's not a problem, and for the rest of the journey he had his hands up like it's fine. I did get really uncomfortable when men stood too close to me and I'd be like can I have a bit of space please, that did bother me.

This connects with Koskela's (2010) notion of 'reasoning', where anxiety is managed by strategies to maintain courage and increase confidence, and how women make the space feel like their own through 'mode and style', projecting the message that they are not afraid. Employing strategies to avoid harassment is part of women's everyday rhythm and movement around the city. They are actioned to such an extent that strategising public space in this way is 'taken-for-granted' (Phadke et al., 2011; Vera-Gray & Kelly, 2020). As Kearl (2010, p. 18) states 'it tends to become a part of their existence and something they must learn to cope with if they want to be able to participate in public life'. Brooks Gardner (1995) considers that even routine pleasures in public space will be experienced with the knowledge of what can occur.

Rachel

Rachel is 31 and has lived in London for the past 10 years. She was travelling back from a work trip in Birmingham to her home in Walthamstow, London. She was heading through an underground tunnel towards the Tube in Euston at around 11 pm. A man asked her for directions, and when she stopped and responded, he accosted her, pushing her against the wall and trying to kiss her. She describes her initial reaction to the incident:

> I was like what the fuck … what's happening and then he grabbed me really hard around my neck, and I was in the tunnel still at this point, it was quiet and then I started struggling, but I was laughing I think out of shock. And also, by that point I … I should say there's context to this, I was quite badly sexually assaulted about 6 months before that … Yeah and I guess smiling is sort of my way of defence in situations like that, like if I come across as friendly and normal then it'll all go away ….

The effects of her previous experience impact her reaction here. As Wilson (1991, p. 102) states: 'we find that the past is not left *as* "past", because individuals carry their pasts around with them'. Wanting the situation to deescalate is congruent to literature that considers sexual harassment as invoking fear of a more severe attack (Gardner et al., 2017; Loukaitou-Sideris & Fink, 2009; Pain, 1991). Therefore, smiling, cooperating and being 'passive' is in fact an active choice. When he wouldn't stop, she describes how she elbowed him in the stomach and told him to leave. She then talks about how she tried to push it out of her mind and carry on with her journey:

> And then I stopped thinking about it. You know that classic thing of pushing it away. It was that thing where you start minimising … I guess, you just think I can't really cope with that being a horrible thing so I'm going to make it a not horrible thing. And you also have to carry on with your life, you don't want to sit there thinking about it all the time … I guess my approach is just let it be over really.

This links to what Jedlowski (2001) describes as the spontaneous process of forgetting what is problematic and painful. It is also resonant of literature that highlights how, as a coping mechanism, women often do not define experiences of sexual assault as such (Roth & Newman, 1991). However, it also highlights an element of resisting the disruption of mobilities by normalising or suppressing the incident itself. Whilst this can be said to play into the normalisation of sexual harassment, it can also be conceptualised as an active decision to minimise disruption to mobilities. Mehta and Bondi (1999) found that women in their research spoke about not letting sexual violence impact or ruin their lives. It is a negotiation that allows the incident to be put into the past, rather than continuing to play an explicit role in the present.

Rachel also talks about how the notion of 'speaking out' or overtly reacting is problematic for her: 'I've tried learning to shout and speak out but it's just not me … And I don't think the burden should be on the person that's experiencing it to have to speak up in a certain way …'. This links with the pressure for women to report experiences of sexual harassment to authorities. There are a number of reasons recognised as limitations on women reporting incidents of sexual harassment in transit (Ceccato, 2017; Gekoski et al., 2015; Loukaitou-Sideris & Fink, 2009; Solymosi et al., 2017). What is often not considered is the implicit message that comes with encouraging women to report sexual harassment. Whilst there are clear benefits that come with reporting (particularly in the long term with regard to policing), it dictates that the burden lies with women to speak out in order for sexual harassment to be combatted. Rachel recognises this saying:

> My friends … said why don't you just speak up and I don't actually find that a supportive response because it makes me feel like I've been really inadequate … and my husband, he was really adamant that I had to report it. And I was so like, why are you blaming me? And he turned it into being a bit about that … but I felt really guilty that I didn't.

Literature that considers the impact of sexual violence in public often focusses on 'space based avoidance' (Ceccato, 2017; d'Arbois de Jubainville & Vanier, 2017, p. 194; Loukaitou-Sideris & Fink, 2009). Memory helps us navigate environments (Foster, 2009), and Rachel's regular use and habitual memories of the space are part of her individual 'map of everyday experience' (Koskela, 2010, p. 309). She retains the knowledge that it is normally a safe space and is therefore able to maintain her regular use of the Tube. For Rachel, although she did not adopt any avoidance behaviours or curtail her physical urban mobilities, the experience was not without spatial implications. Context and space impact the recall of particular memories. Holloway and Hubbard (2001, p. 48) consider how people's images and perceptions of a familiar place remain fairly stable, but acknowledge how a departure from the normal experience can prompt the need for an individual to reassess how they should act and behave within that particular space. Rachel describes how the memory of the incident repeatedly intrudes upon her as she passes through the tunnel where it happened and how this has led her to interact differently in the Tube network:

> I still feel pretty safe on the tube. But I walk through that tunnel
> pretty much every time I commute, and pretty much every time
> I sort of see him in my head, you know. And it's not uncomfort-
> able but I would say that now, in Euston station I note when there
> aren't people around and also, I just wouldn't be friendly to any-
> one, I really wouldn't. I've given up on that.

The way she describes 'seeing him' can be linked to literature on traumatic or emotional memory where mental images of the past spill over into the present (Volkan, 2002, p. 45). Hardy et al. (2009, p. 786) discuss this in regard to sexual assault, where women subsequently experience 'intrusive imagery' and Keightley (2010, p. 57) describes how memory can be an involuntary response to sensory perceptions in the present. Rachel states:

> I still use the tube, but it has a little bit in the sense that I guess
> it just reminds me to always be careful. But it has also made me
> think I'm not going to take this shit anymore, now I've processed
> it I actually now would just go and tell someone.

This links to what Pain (1997, p. 234) described as an 'assiduous state of vigilance' with regard to women's behavioural adaptations. Negotiating space in a mobile environment can become habitual, requiring little attention which can in turn become a source of pleasure (Edensor, 2010). Yet Rachel describes how due to this incident she has now become more wary in this particular space of the London Underground. Whilst habits allow a diminishment of self-monitoring (which women already experience more than men) (Young, 1980), this incident of harassment has taken away both feelings of safety, and automaticity that permit a sense of 'zoning out', relaxation and enjoyment (Urry, 2007), with her urban rhythms consequently becoming disrupted. Rachel says:

> It's so connected to you and your own personal self. And at the
> same time, I wouldn't ever want to stop doing stuff ... so in my
> head there's now a very clear line as to any approach from a man
> in particular that makes me feel threatened, it doesn't matter
> whether or not they thought it was threatening.

Relating to the memory of trauma, Pickering and Keightley (2009, p. 238) consider how the handling of traumatic events can lead to the development of stronger personalities. The subtlety of this links to Lefebvre's (2004) concept of 'secret' or psychological rhythms. Recognising this shows how using fear as a collective way to describe women's reactions can generalise and erase the negotiations such as vigilance and cautiousness or an emboldened use of space.

This chapter has focussed on how the memory of an experience of sexual harassment impacts women's mobilities in the city across space and time. The concept of memory has allowed an exploration as to how a past experience of harassment impacts on present negotiations of urban space and transport, and how both the memory and its impact are renegotiated over time. As time passes women (re)define their experiences, sometimes recognising them only later as sexual harassment or sexual assault. Whilst this recognition caused a sense of being wronged or victimised, this should not be obscured by inducing fear and vulnerability. These accounts show that incidents of sexual harassment and their conceptualisations were often transformed by women into a positive action force in order to make sense of what happened to them and to embolden their claim to public space.

The conceptual framework of rhythms, friction and memory has allowed for a consideration of both the bodily reaction *and* the social, spatial and temporal dynamics at work when women experience sexual harassment, and how these are negotiated over time. The fact that these incidents are happening in a transport environment – a moving space – brings to the forefront the significance of a mobilities perspective in drawing out aspects of these experiences. It becomes clear that immediate reactions to sexual harassment are often shrouded with doubt and uncertainty, shaped by the spatio-temporalities of the Underground and the sociabilities they induce. As time passes these experiences become embedded into women's autobiographical memory (Misztal, 2003). This highlights two key points. Firstly, these experiences act to alter mobilities as the memory reminds women of their potential vulnerability in public space. Secondly, however, these accounts also show that, over time, women can become emboldened by these experiences and use the memory to actively reshape boundaries and claim ownership of their personal space in public spaces.

This chapter has shown that the impact these experiences have on women's mobility is multi-layered, and spatially and temporally implicated. This reveals how sexual harassment forces women to constantly renegotiate their relationship with the city. It is a more subtle undertaking than being instinctively passive or active, disempowered or empowered: the analysis of women's experiences of sexual harassment and its impact over time, shows that there are latitudes between the two. We have seen how, by not simply focussing on female fear of victimisation, we can do justice to the complex negotiations that women incorporate into their lives in order to mitigate men's intrusions that pose a threat to their pleasure and freedom 'on the move'.

Chapter 7

Conclusions: Slowing Down

Abstract

This chapter draws the book to a close by returning to the overarching
goal of this book – to understand women's experiences of sexual harassment on the London Underground. It brings together the key findings
from each chapter. At its core, this book is about deepening and expanding
our understanding of sexual harassment on public transport. However, by
following the continuous thread of gendered mobilities, we can depart from
expected lines of enquiry, broadening our focus to conjoin seemingly disparate conceptual and theoretical approaches and draw out the nuances of
these experiences. So much is revealed through intimate observation of the
seemingly mundane – an empty train carriage, the space between strangers,
and the invisible rhythms that regulate and play out through our corporeal
bodies. This is where we must look to further our enquiries and honour the
complexity of these experiences. Along a similar vein, I hope this book demonstrates the continued need to offer space to women's subjective and experiential stories as a form of rich empirical qualitative data, and how we must
fight for the space and time to do this against the temporal latitudes of the
neoliberal university.

Keywords: Sexual harassment; public transport; London Underground;
rhythmanalysis; qualitative methods; neoliberal university

**Mind the Gender Gap: A Mobilities Perspective of Sexual Harassment on the
London Underground, 113–122**
doi:10.1108/978-1-83753-026-720241007

The Anatomy of Sexual Harassment on the London Underground

The genesis of the idea for the research that constitutes this book grew out of my own experience of a strange man non-consensually rubbing his penis on my back just over a decade ago. Five years later, amid a research project about sexual harassment on public transport, I'm on the top deck of a London bus and a man masturbates at me in broad daylight. My reactions to both incidents left me with an unsettling curdling in my stomach – why didn't I fight back? Why did I just ignore them? Was I scared or confused? Why didn't I care more? Was I a bad feminist? Early on in my research I reached the conclusion that to reduce the mechanisms of sexual harassment on transport to simplistic, environmental (spatial) issues was not enough. This is not a situation that can be understood or fixed by lighting, CCTV, increased policing or crowd management. Similarly, whilst it goes without saying that I agree with work that posits sexual harassment on public transport as symptomatic of patriarchal and sexist social structures and unequal gender relations – I have little new to offer here in terms of theorisation, other than what has been previously summarised. It is a disheartening (and frightening) reality that men continue to harass and abuse women across socio-spatial contexts, and even more so, that this appears to continue without any clear sign of a positive trajectory. However, I hope that this book has at least achieved its primary and most basic aim – to explore, in depth, women's experiences of sexual harassment on the London Underground, and in doing so, demonstrate how the way it is perpetrated and experienced is impacted significantly by the context and space in which these incidents occur. To have a clearer, more nuanced understanding is vital if we are to combat such behaviours.

Transport, and the London Underground specifically, has gradually become recognised as a space where unwanted sexual attention is prolific, so far as being labelled as 'the ultimate hotbed of sexual harassment' (The Standard, 2022). Despite this, there has been scarce research that forensically explores how these incidents play out, and subsequently, theorisations to understand the phenomenon are transferred across from other spaces, assuming similarities and parallels. Yet my own visceral reactions to these experiences told me otherwise. Like many of the women I spoke to, my own reaction surprised me and was incongruent to my sense of self and my anticipated and practised response to sexual harassment in public space. But I also knew that my lack of overt reaction was not simply born out of fear. This was my first inkling that normative interpretations did not always apply to sexual harassment in this environment, and that doing so risked offering misguided and murky explanations.

Through women's in-depth stories, this book aimed to address this gap in knowledge, and illustrate the specificity of these experiences, in comparison to workplace settings, 'the streets' and other public spaces. A significant part of my argument is that these experiences are moulded by the fact that they are happening 'on the move', in a highly kinetic space where rhythms are dictated by seconds not minutes and are disciplined by the flow of capital in the city above. The Underground is a space of nomadism and transition where the social traits of the public realm become compressed and altered in time and space. This book has allowed for an examination of women's mobilities in this liminal situ, showing how the freedom of movement between home, work and leisure continues to be challenged as they temporarily inhabit spaces of transition. The stories presented in this research then, construct the city and the Underground more specifically as a space of tension between freedom of movement, and frictions that are imposed by male travellers and urban tempos. Thus, a mobilities framework around space, time and rhythms has offered a new way of perceiving these intrusions.

The prelude, manifestation and impact of each incident are indeed unique, situated in women's broader urban biographies, yet there are commonalities that weave through these experiences and allow a discernment of the particularities of sexual harassment in a public transport environment. In conversations with women, I often heard my own internal dialogues refracted back at me, and listened to women from disparate backgrounds, with varying experiences, conceptualising and making sense of them in similar ways. I anticipated hearing moderated versions of dominant scripts of sexual harassment – particularly that of the incidents evoking heightened levels of fear and vulnerability – both at the time and subsequently. However, this was quite simply not the case. I initially struggled to avoid partaking in a process of apperception – viewing women's stories through the lens of a presupposed narrative and moulding them to fit my expectations. Indeed, it was very tempting to give more credence and weight to the more invasive incidents, and to the women who had more 'overt' reactions. This, I thought, really shows the impact that sexual harassment has, and justifies its attention. However, this would, of course, dilute the complexity and nuance of these experiences and convolute women's reactions to them. So, with the help of rhythmanalysis, I slowly defamiliarised myself (and hopefully you, as the reader) with how sexual harassment happens and is reacted to on the London Underground. By granularly exploring how women understand these intrusions and allowing space for not just fear, but also anger, confusion, embarrassment and apathy, we can reweave a more nuanced and honest story of journeys of sexual harassment on the London Underground.

Before

In this chapter, we saw women's accounts of everyday life *moving* around London and participating in the rhythmic ensemble of the city. It demonstrated how the city remains a gendered environment that induces both fear and freedom and contextualised the (physical and mental) landscape in which incidents of sexual harassment occur. By using the conceptual character of the flâneur to analyse women's experiences of everyday life in London and of using the Underground, these accounts revealed how the rhythms and sociabilities of the city and the Underground specifically, permitted pleasure, anonymity and freedom, yet concurrently acted to induce isolation and fear. The tensions that exist for women in urban space manifest in relation to the pervasive risk of sexual harassment, which acts as reminder to an underlying apprehension and a need to assess and negotiate one's presence and safety in urban space. However, looking at this through the lens of the flâneur challenges discourses that only express the danger, fear and victimisation that women experience in urban space. Whilst these elements are present, we must not ignore women's complex and practiced negotiations of the multitudinous aspects of urban life that they embody and enact in order to be active, free and if desired, anonymous participants in the city. This chapter showed how the rhythmic attributes of the city and the Underground impacted on women's everyday urban experiences, both permitting them the anonymity to engage in aspects of flânerie, whilst also inducing feelings of stress and isolation. It also demonstrated how the perceived risk and anticipation of sexual violence in public space both contributed to and disrupted their normative rhythms and feelings of freedom in the city, an experience that they recognised as being strongly gendered. This chapter then acted to extend our knowledge of the gendered nature of moving through urban space, and also 'set the scene' for the broader physical, social and psychological landscape in which women experience sexual harassment on the Tube.

During

One of the core contributions of this book is that it has uncovered particularities in the ways in which sexual harassment manifests and is experienced within a transport environment.

The fast-paced rhythms of the city and the sociabilities they induce are just as, if not more, impactful than fear responses. Whilst feminist work has highlighted how sexual harassment happens differently across contexts including the workplace, educational settings and public space (Madan & Nalla, 2016), and mobilities literature has uncovered general behaviours that are specific to transport (Bissell, 2010, 2018; Urry, 2007), connecting these two bodies of work and taking a spatio-temporal approach via the concepts of rhythms (Lefebvre, 2004) and friction (Cresswell, 2010) has allowed conceptual observations to be made as to how sexual harassment manifests and is experienced by women in a public transport environment. Firstly, sexual harassment is shaped by the rhythms of the city that permeate the Underground: the rush hours, lulls and night time, which facilitate and conceal harassment. Secondly, the etiquette and sociabilities on the network, shaped by rhythms, mean that women are often unwilling or anxious about 'making a scene' in an enclosed public space and do not want to disrupt their own urban rhythms and codes of comportment. Thirdly, the transitory nature of the space of the Underground is important, as women often envisage the situation as temporary and act accordingly. The ephemeral nature of the Tube also allows the perpetrator to disappear quickly. Essentially, using a mobilities framework connected incidents of sexual harassment to general time-space structures of the city and the transport network, illustrating how the various rhythms come together to produce a circumstance where particular incidents of harassment are perpetrated. The framework illustrates how harassment is, in part, a spatio-temporal issue, facilitated or hindered by the specific spaces, paces and times of the city. These findings contribute to feminist work that has focussed on how sexual harassment is perpetrated and experienced across contexts, addressing the gap that has existed around public transport environments. It highlights that whilst there are similarities across contexts (e.g. sexual harassment on the streets and in transit is committed by men who are strangers to the victim), there are discerning features that are particular to the transport environment.

After

This chapter provided insight into the impact of sexual harassment and how women negotiate the memories of these experiences over time. When considering the impact of various forms of sexual violence, feminist work has commonly focussed on increased levels of fear (Keane, 1998; Pain, 1991; Stanko, 1995; Warr, 1985). This is also true for work that has looked specifically at the impact of sexual harassment in public space (Gardner, 1995; Kearl, 2010). The findings presented in this book then, permit a move beyond discussing women's access, fear and vulnerability and allow an examination of how sexual harassment in public space is also negotiated and resisted, and how the experiences or memories are also suppressed and act to embolden women. Many of the women whose stories were shared here *did* experience feelings of fear and vulnerability (both at the time of the incident and over time) yet they made active negotiations to resist the impact of sexual harassment on their mobilities. These negotiations were varied, including trying to think as little about the incident as possible; reporting incidents of sexual harassment to authorities; shouting back at harassers in the future in order to claim back ownership of space; and demanding personal space when travelling on the Underground. In contrast, some of the women who did not have an overt response were not 'frozen' out of fear, but seemed to take an apathetic or resigned approach, framing their experiences as 'not a big deal', or 'just one of many'. This chapter, therefore, has contributed to a body of feminist literature that aims to understand fear of violence by taking into account structures of power alongside individual's agency (Koskela, 1997; Mehta & Bondi, 1999). This does not detract from the fact that sexual harassment is experienced as highly intrusive and disruptive (across time) to women's mobilities. Rather it demonstrates women's resistance and ambivalence to the impact of sexual harassment existing alongside, or without fear.

This chapter also demonstrated that the impact sexual harassment has on an individual is not static and unchanging. The concepts of memory, rhythm and friction demonstrated the temporal experience of sexual harassment and how it changes across time and space. By taking this approach, we have explored how the impact on mobility is multi-layered, and spatially and temporally implicated, revealing how sexual harassment forces women to constantly renegotiate their relationship with the city. It is more nuanced than the binaries of being passive and active, disempowered or empowered. The analysis of these women's experiences of sexual harassment and their impact over time shows that there are latitudes between the two. It has shown how not simply focussing on female fear of victimisation can do justice to these negotiations that women incorporate into their lives in order to reduce disruption to their pleasure and freedom in public space. This is a significant contribution to work within the realm of feminist geography that focusses on how women experience and negotiate the city in a gendered way, particularly after experiencing an incident of sexual harassment (Loukaitou-Sideris & Fink, 2009). Using the concept of memory has also highlighted how the incident of harassment itself is remembered differently as time passes. Incidents of sexual harassment or assault can be redefined over time, based on the individual's life trajectory and societal context. The concept of memory then serves to show both the fluidity of the impact of sexual harassment and the fluidity of the memory itself.

The Value of a Mobilities Perspective

This book offers a significant contribution to mobilities studies, a field of work that seeks to address the complexity and impact of social actions and encounters that happen on the move (Sheller & Urry, 2006; Urry, 2000). Conversely, a mobilities perspective has been particularly pertinent for theorising experiences of sexual harassment that are happening in a transport environment: a moving space. The approach permitted an exploration of how the urban and transport rhythms coalesce and intertwine to shape and facilitate the perpetration of, women's experiences of, and responses to, sexual harassment. A mobilities perspective brings to the forefront how these experiences are shaped by the fact they are happening in a mobile environment. A core component of this approach was paying attention to the rhythms of the space, or in Lefebvre's words, rhythmanalysis. Significantly, an attentiveness to rhythms revealed the politics of pace on the network.

Lefebvre's (2004) rhythmanalysis has been employed to look at a multitude of aspects of everyday life in urban space and to explore various social inequalities (Reid-Musson, 2018; Schwanen et al., 2012). Yet to date there is little research that uses a rhythmanalysis perspective to explore gendered experiences or gender inequalities of everyday life in urban space. Lefebvre has been criticised for failing to acknowledge gender inequalities, spatialities and subjectivities in his work (Kipfer et al., 2012; Reid-Musson, 2018), or the non-neutral nature of rhythms. Yet these scholars have also recognised that 'Lefebvre's ideas hold for what might be loosely labelled intersectional research… that seeks to identify gender, sexuality, race and colonial categories of inequality and difference in order to undo them' (Reid-Musson, 2018, p. 885). For this research, rhythmanalysis has provided a framework through which to draw out new insights into the less perceptible aspects of gendered experiences of sexual harassment in a public urban space. The result of this is twofold. Firstly, it demonstrates how navigating city spaces is a highly gendered experience; something remains contested and negotiated. It shows that these negotiations are not solely fear driven, but also shaped by an insistence and resistance, to (re)claim and not be pushed out of public space [or what Koskela (1997) may term 'bold breakings']. Secondly, taking a rhythmanalysis perspective has also permitted a bridge between the corporeal bodily experience of sexual harassment and the role of the broader spatio-temporal dynamics, therefore contributing to feminist discussions regarding how women experience and react to sexual violence in public spaces. It confronts taken for granted ideas of why women react a certain way to sexual harassment within these spaces – again challenging the notion that fear is the dominant regulator. I reiterate, that of course, these experiences of men's intrusions can be fear inducing – that sometimes, they are in fact, terrifying and this fear is well justified. However, rhythmanalysis revealed to me that, alongside experiences of fear, there are other things at play, including confusion, anger, embarrassment and ambivalence. These emotions, themselves induced and shaped by external rhythms, coalesce to mitigate women's responses to sexual harassment in a transport environment.

Something I did not anticipate was how some of the most dominant rhythms at play in shaping these experiences, were the relentless rhythms of capital. At first glance, these temporalities are far removed from the corporeal experience of an incident of sexual harassment, and indeed, they were not immediately articulated by the women I spoke to. However, by endeavouring to grasp and understand the ambivalence with which some of these experiences (including my own) were dealt with, it became clear that, in these moments of intrusion, we are both indelibly human, and simultaneously at the mercy of abstract (capitalist) time that shapes our physical and psycho-political responses. Lefebvre's rhythmanalysis has Marxist roots, so perhaps it is not surprising that, by using this approach to examine the invisible components of experiences of sexual harassment on the Underground, we reveal that it is connected to the temporalities of labour.

As we explored in Chapters 4, 5 and 6, the dominant pace of the Underground, and the behavioural norms it induces, act to enable the perpetration of sexual harassment and mitigate women's responses. I address this by drawing on Baumgartner's (1988) concept of 'moral minimalism'. In the context of this form of social order, she claims that the least extreme reaction to an offence is preferable, and people shy away from exercising explicit social control against each other. This helps us to understand the tussle that often exists between women's autonomy and agency – the desire to react in a way congruent to their sense of self, and the pull of invisible rhythms that force us to act at the bequest of capital by conforming to the temporal policies of the Tube, that encourage silence, and an avoidance of anything that disrupts the journey. In the physical-psycho-spatial nexus of the London Underground carriage, many commuters decidedly disassociate in order to subjectively speed up their journey. Consequently, there is significant disdain towards anything that disrupts this collective condition. Thus, the standardising temporality of the city breeds inertia and apathy in the face of sexual harassment 'on the move'. The dominant temporalities in the space of the Underground reflect standardisation, discipline, surveillance and productivity as some of the most defining elements of our social world. In other words, the structure and perception of time on the Underground, that deeply impact incidents of sexual harassment, reflect the values of time in the city above. To ignore or marginalise the broader context in which these incidents occur is to offer a limited and partial perspective that restricts our understanding.

Final Thoughts – Knowing Sexual Harassment and the Rhythms of Academia

At the core of this book, there are 29 stories derived from in-depth, semi-structured interviews with women who had experienced sexual harassment on the London Underground. These were complemented by countless informal conversations, and my own experiences, observations, fieldnotes and reflexive journal entries, constituting overall in an ethnographic study that spanned across three years. I believe that it is this approach that led to the subtlety of these stories to be rendered conspicuous and permit important new insights into this phenomenon. As such, I want to take the time to reflect on the value of slow and (at times) messy methodologies, and frame them as a positive and important force of friction against the temporal latitudes of neoliberal academia.

In the introductory chapter of this book, I noted how much of the work that has focussed on sexual harassment on transport has been gathered using quantitative approaches and presented in numerical form to offer a rapid assessment or a broad overview (Gekoski et al., 2015; Stringer, 2007). These studies are immensely valuable to assess the scope of the issue; however, through the lens of these methodologies, the complexity of the subjective experience can become simultaneously streamlined and fragmented as it travels from embodied experience, through academic research processes and bureaucracies, and is transformed into a numerical output. Furthermore, the role of context (social, spatial and temporal) in shaping these experiences is often neglected and obscured. As I hope I have illustrated throughout this book, these factors are paramount in understanding the nuance and broader context of these experiences. As such, qualitative methodologies, particularly ethnographic approaches, hold significant value as they take into account the wider social context, as well as offering insight into subjective interpretations, perceptions, beliefs and meanings that women attach to their experiences.

Yet this slow mode of discovery is at risk of becoming marginalised. Over recent decades, academics have documented and warned of the insidious rise of the neoliberal university and its damaging implications. Whereas the liberal university was characterised as a space for slow contemplation and critical thought, the dominant rhythms of contemporary, neoliberal academia are overtly fast paced, driven by commercialisation and marketisation, with a focus on increased performance that is ultimately measurable in economic terms (Troiani & Dutson, 2021). This has been conceptualised in terms of temporalities, and Shaw and Blazek (2023, p. 2) draw on Lefebvre's rhythmanalysis to explore the conflicting rhythms of academic life, arguing that the arrhythmic nature of higher education means it is doomed to a 'slow death' as 'rhythms of crisis-emergency-crisis suck life gradually out of the creativity and functionality of the sector'. Whilst Vostal (2015) argues that 'the fast lane' is not entirely negative, he acknowledges the seriousness of the adverse consequences of a relentless 'rush, hurry and intensified workload for the scholarly profession'. A negative consequence of this at a personal level is the increased pressure to perform, internalisation of a meritocratic ideology and a subsequent mutation of the academic self, and possible burn out. In the gym of academic metrics [or what Beer (2016) terms 'metric power'], publishing mantras, grant imperatives and Research Excellence Frameworks, we are stewarded onto a treadmill that sculpts our academic identities into apparatus through which the ideologies and priorities of the academy are performed. In this landscape, as the title of Menzies and Newson (2007) article suggests, academics are often left with 'no time to think'.

This may seem like an unnecessary diversion at this point in the book; however, it is a dominant institutional *rhythm* that poses broader epistemological concerns. The academic 'need for speed' in the production of knowledge endangers the effective use of qualitative methodologies, and as such, our ability to form useful, impactful understandings of complex social issues. It has been well documented that, in the context described above, quantitative approaches are deemed more valuable due to their fast, 'scientific' outputs, with 'real world' application and economic benefits, in comparison to slow and 'messy' qualitative approaches. This implicates whose voices are heard, how they are amplified (or quashed) and how much time is taken to understand what is being said. In the context of this book, for example, I am adamant that the relatively slow and messy way in which knowledge was gathered led to the formation of a valuable conceptual framework, that I have argued throughout, offers a new perspective on sexual harassment on public transport. Long, muddled conversations over coffee and endless hours going nowhere in particular on the Tube, observing and 'sensing' the atmospheres and rhythms of the space, offered a wealth of complex and often contradictory data. I had time to read up on interesting, yet seemingly unconnected concepts, and I had space to laterally theorise and make sense of the data – rather than a time frame (or supervisor) nudging me to diminish its complexity. I contend that working to these unhurried rhythms permitted me to challenge, shift and strengthen our understandings of how sexual harassment is experienced on public transport.

If this slow mode of researching and 'thinking' is in jeopardy in the context of the university, then we risk participating in a process of misguided epistemological reductionism and theoretical apperception. By limiting the scope of methodologies academics are able to feasibly employ [whilst striving to be 'world leading' researchers, 'excellent' teachers and professional administrators (Feldman & Sandoval, 2018)], the complex, subjective knowledge of the experiences of (in this case) sexual harassment themselves become out of reach, pushed to the fringes of our consciousness, and remains known only at the individual corporeal and psychological level of the victim. This is hugely problematic, with very real implications – it is in this reductive and shallow ontological realm, that experiences that are part of a broader phenomenon become atomised, fragmented and individualised. And, it is from this limited and linear understanding, whether born out of naivete, ignorance or an active disavowal of anything too complex and systemic, that simplistic policies and practices are justified. In the context of sexual harassment and gender-based violence, we see this process rear its head in the amplification of shallow recommendations, for example, when we see perpetrators being framed as 'bad apples' and punished punitively, and women being victim blamed for taking risks and encouraged to engage in more safety work.

In this context, any broader social factors at play are misunderstood or neglected entirely.

The depth of what we 'know' of sexual harassment, who perpetrates it, and how victims experience and deal with the impact of these intrusions, should not be diminished at the mercy of institutional academic rhythms. There is a balance to be made between the demand for rapid results, and the need for nuanced understandings of complex social issues, but the power of the pace of a neoliberal university first requires acknowledgement in order to enact some form of resistance. Menzies and Newson (2007, p. 83) urge academics to 'champion temporal practices which allow time for the "deep presence" required for creative intellectual work. As an early career researcher, I am writing this, in part, as a reminder to myself to resist 'unconscious submission' (Clarke & Knights, 2015) to the rhythms of the university. As Lefebvre contends, rhythms have the power to reveal the politics of pace – and here, efficiency and speed perpetuate the inducement of moral minimalism across social spheres. Now more than ever, I contend that it is vital to slow down, and to feel and understand the rhythms of women's complex and messy experiences of men's intrusions in urban space. In order to carve out the opportunities to mobilise these often suppressed forms of knowledge, we must create our own rhythms, demand the time to listen, and the space to think!

References

Adam, B. (1991). *Time and social theory*. Temple University Press.

Addams, J. (2002/1916). *The long road of woman's memory*. University of Chicago Press.

Adey, P. (2006). If mobility is everything then it is nothing: Towards a relational politics of (im)mobilities. *Mobilities*, *1*(1), 75–94. https://doi.org/10.1080/17450100500489080

Ahmed, S. (2004). *The cultural politics of emotion*. Edinburgh University Press.

Anderson, L. (2006). Analytic autoethnography. *Journal of Contemporary Ethnography*, *35*(4), 373–395. https://doi.org/10.1177/0891241605280449

Augé, M. (1995). *Non-places: Introduction to an anthropology of supermodernity*. Verso.

Bailey, B. (2017). Piropo as a cultural term for talk in the Spanish-speaking world. In D. Carbaugh (Ed.). *Handbook of communication in cross-cultural perspective* (p. 44). Routledge. https://scholarworks.umass.edu/communication_faculty_pubs/44

Bailey, M., & Trudy (2018). On misogynoir: Citation, erasure, and plagiarism. *Feminist Media Studies*, *18*(4), 762–768. https://doi.org/10.1080/14680777.2018.1447395

Ball, K., Wesson, C. J. (2017). Perceptions of unwanted sexual behaviour on public transport: Exploring transport density and behaviour severity. *Crime Prevention and Community Safety*, *19*(3–4), 199–201.

Bancroft, K. (2002). Zones of exclusion: Urban spatial policies, social justice, and social services. *Journal of Sociology and Welfare*, *39*(3), 63–84. https://doi.org/10.15453/0191-5096.3684

Barrow, R. J. (2015). Rape on the railway: Women, safety, and moral panic in Victorian newspapers. *Journal of Victorian Culture*, *20*(3), 341–356. https://doi.org/10.1080/13555502.2015.1057390

Baudelaire, C. (1964). The painter of modern life. *The painter of modern life and other essays*. Phaidon Press.

Baumgartner, M. P. (1988). *The moral order of a suburb*. Oxford University Press.

Beck, U., & Sznaider, N. (2006) Unpacking cosmopolitanism for the social sciences: A research agenda. *British Journal of Sociology*. *57*(1), 1–23. https://doi.org/10.1111/j.1468-4446.2006.00091.x

Beer, D. (2016). Metric Power. Palgrave Macmillian.

Benjamin, W. (1968). *Illuminations: Essays and reflections*. Schoken Books.

Benjamin, W. (1982). *The Arcades Project*. Harvard University Press.

Bilge, S. (2010). Recent feminist outlooks on intersectionality. *Diogenes*, *57*(1), 58–72. https://doi.org/10.1177/0392192110374245

Binnie, J., & Skeggs, B. (2004). Cosmopolitan knowledge and the production and consumption of sexualized space: Manchester's gay village. *The Sociological Review*, *52*(1), 39–61. https://doi.org/10.1111/j.1467-954X.2004.00441.x

Bissell, D. (2009). Travelling vulnerabilities: Mobile timespaces of quiescence. *Cultural Geographies*, *16*(4), 427–445. http://www.jstor.org/stable/44251292

Bissell, D. (2010). Passenger mobilities: Affective atmospheres and the sociality of public transport. *Environment and Planning D: Society and Space*, *28*(2), 270–289. https://doi.org/10.1068/d3909

Bissell, D. (2018). *Transit life: How commuting is transforming our cities*. MIT Press.

Bleakley, P. (2023). "Would your level of disgust change?" Accounting for variant reactions to fatal violence against women on social media. *Criminology & Criminal Justice*, *23*(5), 845–860. https://doi.org/10.1177/17488958221105155

Bondestam, F., & Lundqvist, M. (2020). Sexual harassment in higher education – A systematic review. *European Journal of Higher Education*, *10*(4), 397–419. https://doi.org/10.1080/21568235.2020.1729833

Bondurant, A. B. (2001). University women's acknowledgement of rape: Individual, interpersonal, and social factors. *Violence Against Women*, *7*(3), 294–314. https://doi.org/10.1177/1077801201007003004

Bookman, A., & Morgen, S. (1987). *Women, politics and empowerment: Women in the political economy*. Temple University Press.

Botta, R. A., & Pingree, S. (1997). Interpersonal communication and rape: Women acknowledge their assaults. *Journal of Health Communication*, *2*(3), 197–212. https://doi.org/10.1080/108107397127752

Boutin, A. (2012). Rethinking the Flâneur: Flânerie and the senses. *Dix-Neuf*, *16*(2), 124–132. https://doi.org/10.1179/dix.2012.16.2.01

Boutros, M. (2018). A multidimensional view of legal cynicism: Perceptions of the police among anti-harassment teams in Egypt. *Law & Society Review*, *52*(2), 368–400.

Bowman, C. G. (1993). Street harassment and the informal ghettoization of women. *Harvard Law Review*, *106*(3), 517–580.

Bows, H., Day, A., & Dhir, A. (2024). "It's like a drive by misogyny": Sexual violence at UK music festivals. *Violence Against Women*, *30*(2), 372–393. https://doi.org/10.1177/10778012221120443

Bows, H., & Westmarland, N. (2017). Rape of older people in the United Kingdom: Challenging the 'real-rape' stereotype. *The British Journal of Criminology*, *57*(1), 1–17. https://doi.org/10.1093/bjc/azv116

Boyd, A., & McEwan, B. (2022). Viral paradox: The intersection of "me too" and #MeToo. *New Media & Society*, *26*(6), 3454–3471. https://doi.org/10.1177/14614448221099187

Boyer, K. (2022). Sexual harassment and the right to everyday life. *Progress in Human Geography*, *46*(2), 398–415. https://doi.org/10.1177/03091325211024340

Bradbury-Jones, C., Appleton, J. V., Clark, M., Paavilainen, E. (2019). A profile of gender-based violence research in Europe: Findings from a focused mapping review and synthesis. *Trauma, Violence, & Abuse*, *20*(4), 470–483. https://doi.org/10.1177/1524838017719234

Brant, C., & Lee Too, Y. (1994). *Rethinking sexual harassment*. Pluto Press.

Brooks Gardner, C. (1995). *Passing by, gender and public harassment*. University of California Press.

Brownmiller, S. (1975). *Against our will: Men, women and rape*. Simon & Schuster.

Campbell, R., Adams, A., Wasco, S., Ahrens, C., & Sefl, T. (2009). Training interviewers for research on sexual violence: A qualitative study of rape survivors' recommendations for interview practice. *Violence Against Women*, *15*(5), 595–617. https://doi.org/10.1177/1077801208331248

Carastathis, A. (2014). The concept of intersectionality in feminist theory. *Philosophy Compass*, *9*(5), 304–314. https://doi.org/10.1111/phc3.12129

Carroll, K. (2012). Infertile? The emotional labour of sensitive and feminist research methodologies, *Qualitative Research*, *13*(5), 546–561. https://doi.org/10.1177/1468794112455039

Caruth, C. (Ed). (1995). *Trauma: Explorations in memory*. Johns Hopkins University Press.

Carver, A., & Veitch, J. (2020). Perceptions and patronage of public transport – Are women different from men? *Journal of Transport and Health*, *19*, 1–7. https://doi.org/10.1016/J.JTH.2020.100955

Catalano, S., Smith, E., Snyder, H., & Rand, M. (2009). *Female victims of violence*. U.S. Department of Justice Publications and Materials. https://digitalcommons.unl.edu/usjusticematls/7

Ceccato, V. (2017). Women's victimisation and safety in transit environments. *Crime Prevention and Community Safety*, *19*(3), 163–167. https://doi.org/10.1057/s41300-017-0024-5

Ceccato, V., Gaudelet, N., & Graf, G. (2022). Crime and safety in transit environments: A systematic review of the English and the French literature, 1970–2020. *Public Transport, 14*, 105–153. https://doi.org/10.1007/s12469-021-00265-1

Ceccato, V., & Paz, Y. (2017). Crime in São Paulo's metro system: Sexual crimes against women. *Crime Prevention and Community Safety, 19*, 211–226. https://doi.org/10.1057/s41300-017-0027-2

Ceccato, V., & Uittenbogaard, A. C. (2014). Space-time dynamics of crime in transport nodes. *Annals of the Association of American Geographers, 104*(1), 131–150. http://www.jstor.org/stable/24537741

Chaney, D. (1983). The department store as a cultural form. *Theory, Culture and Society, 1*(3), 22–31. https://doi.org/10.1177/026327648300100303

Chowdhury, R. (2023). Sexual assault on public transport: Crowds, nation, and violence in the urban commons. *Social & Cultural Geography, 24*(7), 1087–1103. https://doi.org/10.1080/14649365.2022.2052170.

Clarke, C., & Knights, D. (2015). Careering through academia: Securing identities or engaging ethical subjectivities?. *Humans Relations, 68*(12), 1865–1888. https://doi.org/10.1177/0018726715570978

Cleere, C., & Lynn, S. J. (2013). Acknowledged versus unacknowledged sexual assault among college women. *Journal of Interpersonal Violence, 28*(12), 2593–2611. https://doi.org/10.1177/0886260513479033

Cohen, L., & Felson, M. (1979). Social change and crime rate trends: A routine activity approach. *American Sociological Review, 44*(4), 588–608. https://doi.org/10.2307/2094589

Connell, R. W. (1995). *Masculinities*. University of California Press.

Cortina, L., & Areguin, M. A. (2021). Putting people down and pushing them out: Sexual harassment in the workplace. *Annual Review of Organizational Psychology and Organizational Behaviour, 8*, 285–309. https://doi.org/10.1146/annurev-orgpsych-012420-055606

Crang, M. (2001). Temporalised space and motion. In J. May & N. Thrift (Eds.), *Timespace: Geographies of temporality* (pp. 187–207). Routledge.

Cregan, K. (2006). *The sociology of the body*. Sage Publications.

Crenshaw, K. (1989). Demarginalizing the intersection of race and sex: A black feminist critique of antidiscrimination doctrine, feminist theory and antiracist politics. *University of Chicago Legal Forum, 1989*(1), Article 8. http://chicagounbound.uchicago.edu/uclf/vol1989/iss1/8

Cresswell, T. (2010). Towards a politics of mobility. *Environment and Planning D: Society and Space, 28*(1), 17–31. https://doi.org/10.1068/d11407

Cresswell, T. (2014). Friction. In P. Adey, D. Bissell, K. Hannam, P. Merriman, & M. Sheller (Eds.), *The Routledge handbook of mobilities* (pp. 107–115). Routledge.

Crouch, M, (2009). Sexual harassment in public places. *Social Philosophy Today. Gender, Diversity and Difference, 25*, 137–148.

Cuenca-Piqueras, C., Fernández-Prados, J. S., & González-Moreno, M. J. (2023). Approach to theoretical perspectives of "sexual harassment": Review and bibliometric analysis from social sciences. *Frontiers in Psychology, 18*(14), 1088469. https://doi.org/10.3389/fpsyg.2023.1088469

d'Arbois de Jubainville, H., & Vanier, C. (2017). Women's avoidance behaviours in public transport in the Ile-de-France region. *Crime Prevention and Community Safety, 19*(3–4), 183–198. https://doi.org/10.1057/s41300-017-0023-6

De Becker, G. (2000). *The gift of fear*. Bloomsbury Publishing.

DeVault, M. L. (1996). Talking back to sociology: Distinctive contributions of feminist methodology. *Annual Review of Sociology, 22*, 29–50. http://www.jstor.org/stable/2083423

Dhillon, M., & Bakaya, S. (2014). Street harassment: A qualitative study of the experiences of young women in Delhi. *SAGE Open*, *4*(3), 1–11. https://doi.org/10.1177/2158244014543786

Di Gennaro, K., & Ritschel, C. (2019). Blurred lines: The relationship between catcalls and compliments. *Women's Studies International Forum*, *75*, 102239. https://doi.org/10.1016/j.wsif.2019.102239

Ding, H., Loukaitou-Sideris, A., & Agrawal, A. W. (2020). Sexual harassment and assault in transit environments: A review of the English-language literature. *Journal of Planning Literature*, *35*(3), 267–280. https://doi.org/10.1177/0885412220911129

Dobash, R. E., & Dobash, R. (1979). *Violence against wives: A case against the patriarchy.* Free Press.

Dobbs, L. (2005). Wedded to the car: Women, employment and the importance of private transport. *Transport Policy*, *12*(3), 266–278. https://doi.org/10.1016/j.tranpol.2005.02.004

Doherty, J., Busch-Geertsema, V., Karpuskiene, V., Korhonen, J., O'Sullivan E., Sahlin, I., Tosi, A., Petrillo, A., & Wygnańska, J. (2008). Homelessness and exclusion: Regulating public space in European cities. *Surveillance and Society*, *5*(3), 290–314.

Dunier, M., Kasinitz, P., & Murphy, A. (2014). *The urban ethnography reader*. Oxford University Press.

Edensor, T. (Ed.). (2010). *Geographies of rhythm: Nature, place, mobilities and bodies.* Routledge. https://doi.org/10.4324/9781315584430

Edensor, T. (2011). Commuter: Mobility rhythm and commuting. In T. Cresswell & P. Merriman (Eds.), *Geographies of mobilities: Practices, spaces, subjects* (pp. 189–204). Routledge.

Elkin, L. (2016). *Flâneuse: Women walk the city in Paris, New York, Tokyo, Venice and London.* Chatto & Windus.

Farley, L. (1978). *Sexual shakedown: The sexual harassment of women on the job.* McGraw-Hill.

Feldman, Z., & Sandoval, M. (2018) Metric power and the academic self: Neoliberalism, knowledge and resistance in the British university. *Journal for a Global Sustainable Information Society*, *16*(1), 214–233. https://doi.org/10.31269/triplec.v16i1.899

Felski, R. (1995). *The gender of modernity.* Harvard University Press.

Felson, M., de Melo, S. N., & Boivin, R. (2021). Risk of outdoor rape and proximity to bus stops, bars, and residences. *Violence and Victims*, *36*(6), 723–738.

Felson, M., Boba, R. L., Clarke, R. V., & Wiesburd, D. (1994). *Diffusion of crime control benefits: Observations on the reverse of displacement.* In R. V. Clarke (Ed.), *Crime prevention studies* (Vol. 2, pp. 165–183). Lynne Rienner.

Ferraro, K. F. (1996). Women's fear of victimization: Shadow of sexual assault? *Social Forces*, *75*(2), 667–690.

Fileborn, B. (2016). *Reclaiming the night-time economy. Unwanted sexual attention in pubs and clubs.* Palgrave Macmillan.

Fileborn, B. (2019). Naming the unspeakable harm of street harassment: A survey-based examination of disclosure Practices. *Violence Against Women*, *25*(2), 223–248. https://doi.org/10.1177/1077801218768709

Fileborn, B., & O'Neill, T. (2023). From "Ghettoization" to a field of its own: A comprehensive review of street harassment research. *Trauma, Violence, & Abuse*, *24*(1), 125–138. https://doi.org/10.1177/15248380211021608

Fineran, S., & Bennett, L. (1999). Gender and power issues of peer sexual harassment among teenagers. *Journal of Interpersonal Violence*, *14*(6), 626–641. https://doi.org/10.1177/088626099014006004

Fisher, B. S., Daigle, L. E., Cullen, F. T., & Turner, M. G. (2003). Acknowledging sexual victimization as rape: Results from a national-level survey. *Justice Quarterly*, *20*(3), 535–574. https://doi.org/10.1080/07418820300095611

Fitzgerald, L. F., & Buchanan, N. T. (2008). Effects of racial and sexual harassment on work and the psychological well-being of African American women. *Journal of Occupational. Health Psychology*, *13*, 137–151. https://doi.org/10.1037/1076-8998. 13.2.137

Fogg-Davis, H. G. (2006). Theorizing black lesbians within black feminism: A critique of same-race street harassment. *Politics & Gender*, *2*(1), 57–76. https://doi.org/ 10.1017/S1743923X06060028

Foster, J. K. (2009). *Memory: A very short introduction*. Oxford University Press.

Frisby, D. (1994). The flâneur in social theory. In K. Tester (Ed.), *The flâneur* (pp. 81–110). Routledge.

Gardner, N., Cui, J., & Coiacetto, E. (2017). Harassment on public transport and its impact on women's travel behaviour. *Australian Planner*, *54*(46), 1–8. https://doi.org/ 10.1080/07293682.2017.1299189

Gartman, D. (2004). Three ages of the automobile: The cultural logics of the car. *Theory, Culture and Society*, *21*(4–5), 169–196. https://doi.org/10.1177/0263276404046066

Gekoski, A., Gray, J. M., Horvath, M. A. H., Edwards, S., Emirali, A., & Adler, J. R. (2015). *'What works' in reducing sexual harassment and sexual offences on public transport nationally and internationally: A rapid evidence assessment*. British Transport Police and Department for Transport.

Gelsthorpe, L., & Morris, A. (Eds.). (1990). *Feminist perspectives in criminology*. Open University Press.

Giddens, A. (1990). *The consequences of modernity*. Polity Press.

Gilchrist, E., Bannister, J., Ditton, J., & Farrall, S. (1998). Women and the 'fear of crime': Challenging the accepted stereotype. *British Journal of Criminology*, *38*(2), 283–298. http://www.jstor.org/stable/23638718

Gilligan, C. (1990). Joining the resistance: Psychology, politics, girls and women. *Michigan Quarterly Review*, *29*, 501–526.

Gleber, A. (1998). *The art of taking a walk: Flânerie, literature, and film in Weimar culture*. Princeton University Press.

Goffman, E. (1955). On face-work: An analysis of ritual elements in social interaction. *Psychiatry*, *18*(3), 213–231.

Goffman, E. (1963). *Behaviour in public places: Notes on the social organization of gatherings*. Free Press.

Goffman, E. (1971). *Relations in public; microstudies of the public order*. Basic Books.

Gottdiener, M., & Huthinson, R. (2006). *The new urban sociology*. Avalon Publishing.

Graves-Brown, P. M. (2000). Always crashing in the same car. In P. M. Graves-Brown (Ed.), *Matter, materiality and modern culture* (pp. 155–163). Routledge.

Green, J. F. (2022). Smashing backdoors in and the wandering eye: An introduction to Bartenders' experiences with unwanted sexual attention while working in the UK. *Feminist Criminology*, *17*(1), 96–115. https://doi.org/10.1177/15570851211001922

Gruber, J. (1998). The impact of male work environments and organizational policies on women's experiences of sexual harassment. *Gender and Society*, *3*(12), 301–320. http://www.jstor.org/stable/190287

Gunby, C., Carline, A., Taylor, S., & Gosling, H. (2020). Unwanted sexual attention in the night-time economy: Behaviors, safety strategies, and conceptualizing "feisty femininity". *Feminist Criminology*, *15*(1), 24–46. https://doi.org/10.1177/1557085 119865027

Halbwachs, M. (1950). *The collective memory* (F. J. Ditter, V. Y. Ditter, Trans., M. Douglas, introd.). Harper Colophon.

Hand, J., & Sanchez, L. (2000). Badgering or bantering? Gender differences in experience of, and reactions to, sexual harassment among U.S high school students. *Gender and Society*, *14*(6), 718–746. https://doi.org/10.1177/089124300014006002

Hannam, K., Sheller, M., & Urry, J. (2006). Editorial: Mobilities, immobilities and moorings. *Mobilities, 1*(1), 1–22, https://doi.org/10.1080/17450100500489189

Hardy, A., Young, K., & Holmes, E. A. (2009). Does trauma memory play a role in the experience of reporting sexual assault during police interviews? An exploratory study. *Memory, 17*(8), 783–788. https://doi.org/10.1080/09658210903081835

Havas, J., & Horeck, T. (2021). Netflix feminism: Binge-watching rape culture in unbreakable Kimmy Schmidt and unbelievable. In M. Jenner (Ed.), *Binge-watching and contemporary television studies* (pp. 250–273). Edinburgh University Press. https://doi.org/10.3366/edinburgh/9781474461986.003.0017

Henry, N., Flynn, A., & Powell, A. (2020). *Technology-facilitated domestic and sexual violence: A review. Violence Against Women, 26*(15–16), 1828–1854. https://doi.org/10.1177/1077801219875821

Herbel, S., & Gaines, D. (2009). *Women's issue in transportation: Summary of the 4th international conference* (Vol. 2). Transportation Research Board. https://doi.org/10.17226/22887

Hlavka, H. R. (2014). Normalizing sexual violence: Young women account for harassment and abuse. *Gender & Society, 28*(3), 337–358. https://doi.org/10.1177/0891243214526468

Highmore, B. (2002). Street life in London: Towards a rhythmanalysis of London in the late nineteenth century. *New Formations. 47*, 171–193.

Hill Collins, P. (1986). Learning from the outsider within: The sociological significance of black feminist thought. *Social Problems, 33*(6), 14–32. https://doi.org/10.2307/800672

Hobbs, D., Lister, S., Hadfield, P., & Winlow, S. (2005). Violence and control in the night-time economy. *European Journal of Crime, Criminal Law and Criminal Justice, 13*(1), 89–102. https://doi.org/10.1163/1571817053558310

Holloway, L., & Hubbard, P. (2001). *People and place: The extraordinary geographies of everyday life*. Pearson Education.

Holt, A., & Lewis, S. (2024). A sense of danger: Gender-based violence and the quest for a sensory criminology. *Feminist Criminology, 19*(1), 3–24. https://doi.org/10.1177/15570851231207866

Hooks, B. (1981). *Ain't I a woman: Black women and feminism*. Pluto Press.

Horii, M., & Burgess. A. (2012). Constructing sexual risk: 'Chikan', collapsing male authority and the emergence of women-only train carriages in Japan. *Health, Risk & Society, 14*(1), 41–55. https://doi.org/10.1080/13698575.2011.641523

Hornsey, R. (2012). Listening to the tube map: Rhythm and the historiography of urban map use. *Environment and Planning D: Society and Space, 30*(4), 675–693. https://doi.org/10.1068/d1410

Hubbard, P. (2001). Sex zones: Intimacy, citizenship and public space. *Sexualities, 4*(1), 51–71. https://doi.org/10.1177/136346001004001003

Hubbard, P. (2012). *Cities and sexualities*. Routledge.

Hubbard, P., & Lilley, K. (2004). Pacemaking in the modern city: The urban politics of speed and slowness. *Environment and Planning D: Society and Space, 22*(2), 273–294. https://doi.org/10.1068/d338t

Ingold, T. (2007). *Lines: A brief history*. Routledge.

Ison, J., Forsdike, K., Henry, N., Hooker, L., & Taft, A. (2023). "You're just constantly on alert": Women and gender-diverse people's experiences of sexual violence on public transport. *Journal of Interpersonal Violence, 38*(21–22), 11617–11641. https://doi.org/10.1177/08862605231186123

Jackson, P. (1985). Urban ethnography. *Progress in Human Geography, 9*(2), 157–176. https://doi.org/10.1177/030913258500900201

Jaffe, A. E., Steel, A. L., DiLillo, D. D., Messman-Moore, T. L., & Gratz, K. L. (2017). Characterizing sexual violence in intimate relationships: An examination of blame attributions and rape acknowledgement. *Journal of Interpersonal Violence, 36*(1–2), 469–490. https://doi.org/10.1177/0886260517726972

Jedlowski, P. (2001). Memory and sociology: Themes and issues. *Time & Society*, *10*(1), 29–44. https://doi.org/10.1177/0961463X01010001002

Jenks, C., & Neves, T. (2000). A walk on the wild side: Urban ethnography meets the flâneur, *Cultural Values*, *4*(1), 1–17, https://doi.org/10.1080/14797580009367183

Kahn, A. S., Jackson, J., Kully, C., Badger, K., & Halvorsen, J. (2003). Calling it rape: Differences in experiences of women who do or do not label their sexual assault as rape. *Psychology of Women Quarterly*, *27*(3), 233–242. https://doi.org/10.1111/1471-6402.00103

Karandikar, S. Munshi, A., & Cho, H. (2024). "Say something in your language": Lived experiences of Asian Americans during the COVID-19 pandemic. *Asian Social Work and Policy Review*, *18*(1), e12293. https://doi.org/10.1111/aswp.12293

Kavanaugh, P. R. (2013). The continuum of sexual violence: Women's accounts of victimization in urban nightlife. *Feminist Criminology*, *8*(1), 20–39. https://doi.org/10.1177/1557085112442979

Keane, C. (1995). Victimization and fear: Assessing the role of the offender and the offence. *Canadian Journal of Criminology*, *37*(3), 431–455. https://doi.org/10.3138/cjcrim.37.3.431

Keane, C. (1998). Evaluating the influence of fear of crime as an environmental mobility restrictor on women's routine activities. *Environment and Behaviour*, *30*(1), 60–74. https://doi.org/10.1177/0013916598301003

Kearl, H. (2010). *Stop street harassment: Making public places safe and welcoming for women*. Praeger.

Keightley, E. (2010). Remembering research: Memory and methodology in the social sciences. *International Journal of Social Research and Memory*, *13*(1), 55–70. https://doi.org/10.1080/13645570802605440

Kelly, L. (1987). *The continuum of sexual violence in women*. In J. Hanmer, & M. Maynard (Eds.), *Violence and social control* (pp. 46–60). MacMillian Press Ltd.

Kelly, L. (1988). *Surviving sexual violence. Feminist perspectives series*. University of Minnesota Press.

Kimmel, M. (2008). *Guyland: The perilous world where boys become men*. Harper Collins.

Kipfer, S., Saberi, P., Wieditz, T. (2012). Henri Lefebvre: Debates and controversies. *Progress in Human Geography*, *37* (1), 115–134.

Koskela, H. (1997). 'Bold walk and breakings': Women's spatial confidence versus fear of violence. *Gender, Place and Culture*, *4*(3), 301–320. http://dx.doi.org/10.1080/09663699725369

Koskela, H. (1999). Gendered exclusions: Women's fear of violence and changing relations to space. *Geografiska Annaler. Series B, Human Geography*, *81*(2), 111–124. http://www.jstor.org/stable/491020

Koskela, H. (2010). Fear and its others. In S. Smith, R. Pain, S. A. Marston, & J. P. Jones, III (Eds.), *The SAGE handbook of social geographies* (pp. 389–407). Sage Publications.

Krasas, J. R., & Henson, K. (1997). "Hey, why don't you wear a shorter skirt?": Structural vulnerability and the organization of sexual harassment in temporary clerical employment. *Gender and Society*, *11*(2), 215–237. http://www.jstor.org/stable/3081845

Larsen, J., Axhausen, K. W., & Urry, J. (2006) Geographies of social networks: Meetings, travel and communications. *Mobilities*, *1*(2), 261–283. https://doi.org/10.1080/17450100600726654

Le Bon, G. (2004). *The crowd: A study of the popular mind*. Kessinger Publishing.

Leder, D. (1990). *The absent body*. The University of Chicago Press.

Lefebvre, H. (1991). *The production of space*. Wiley-Blackwell.

Lefebvre, H. (2004). *Rhythmanalysis, space, time and everyday life*. Bloomsbury Publishing.

Lersch, K. M., & Hart, T. C. (2023). Does routine activity theory still matter during COVID-19 restrictions? The geography of sexual assaults before, during, and after COVID-19 restrictions. *Journal of Criminal Justice*, *86*, 102050. https://doi.org/10.1016/j.jcrimjus.2023.102050

Levin, L. (2019). How may public transport influence the practice of everyday life among younger and older people and how may their practices influence public transport? *Social Sciences, 8*(3), 96. https://doi.org/10.3390/socsci8030096

Lewis, S. (2023). 'We call it getting your eye in': Policing sexual harassment on the London Underground through the lens of Haraway's situated knowledges and cyborgs. *The British Journal of Criminology, 63*(5), 1129–1145. https://doi.org/10.1093/bjc/azac080

Lewis, S., Saukko, P., & Lumsden, K. (2021). Rhythms, sociabilities and transience of sexual harassment in transport: Mobilities perspectives of the London underground, *Gender, Place & Culture, 28*(2), 277–298. https://doi.org/10.1080/0966369X.2020.1734540

Lim, L. (2002). Sexual assaults in Singapore: A comparative study of rapists and molesters. *Medicine, Science and the Law, 42*(4), 344–350.

Little, J. (1994). *Gender, planning and the policy process*. Pergamon.

Lorde, A. (1984). *Sister outsider: Essays and speeches*. Ten Speed Press.

Loukaitou-Sideris, A. (1999). Hot spots of bus stop crime: The importance of environmental attributes. *Journal of the American Planning Association, 65*(4), 395–341. https://doi.org/10.1080/01944369908976070

Loukaitou-Sideris, A., & Ceccato, V. (2020). Sexual harassment on transit: Evidence from the literature. In V. Ceccato & A. Loukaitou-Sideris (Eds.), *Transit crime and sexual violence in cities: International evidence and prevention* (pp. 12–23). Taylor & Francis Group.

Loukaitou-Sideris, A., & Fink, C. (2009). Addressing women's fear of victimization in transportation settings: A survey of U.S transit agencies. *Urban Affairs Review, 44*(4), 554–587. https://doi.org/10.1177/1078087408322874

Loukaitou-Sideris, A. (2014). Fear and safety in transit environments from the women's perspective. *Security Journal, 27*(2), 242–256.

Lumsden, K. (2009). *Rebels of the road: A sociological analysis of Aberdeen's 'Boy Racer' culture and the societal reaction to their behaviour* [Doctoral dissertation, University of Aberdeen. Scotland].

Lumsden, K. (2015). (Re) civilizing the young driver: Technization and emotive automobility. *Mobilities, 10*(1), 36–54. https://doi.org/10.1080/17450101.2013.823716

Lynch, K. (1960). *The image of the city*. MIT Press.

Lyons, G., & Urry, J. (2005). Travel time use in the information age. *Transportation Research Part A Policy and Practice, 39*(2–3), 257–276. https://doi.org/10.1016/j.tra.2004.09.004

Lynes, A., Kelly, C., & Uppal, P. K. S. (2019). Benjamin's 'flâneur' and serial murder: An ultra-realist literary case study of Levi Bellfield. *Crime, Media, Culture, 15*(3), 523–543. https://doi.org/10.1177/1741659018815934

MacKinnon, C.A. (1979). *Sexual harassment of working women: A case of sex discrimination*. Yale University Press.

MacKinnon, C. A., & Siegel, R. (2004). *Directions in sexual harassment law*. Yale University Press.

Madan, M., & Nalla, M. (2016). Sexual harassment in public spaces: Examining perceived seriousness and victimization. *International Criminal Justice Review, 26*(2), 80–97. https://doi.org/10.1177/1057567716639093

Madriz, E. (1997). *Nothing good happens to good girls*. University of California Press.

Malone, K., & Hasluck, L. (1998). Geographies of exclusion: young people's perceptions and use of public space. *Family Matters* (49), 20–26.

Marcela Quinones, L. (2020). Sexual harassment in public transport in Bogotá. *Transportation Research Part A: Policy and Practice, 139*, 54–69. https://doi.org/10.1016/j.tra.2020.06.018

Marston, S., Jones, J. P., & Woodward, K. (2005). Human geography without scale. *Royal Geographical Society (with the Institute of British Geographers)*, *30*(4), 416–432. http://www.jstor.org/stable/3804505

Mason, J. (2002). *Qualitative researching*. Sage Publications.

Mason-Bish, H., & Zempi, I. (2019). Misogyny, racism, and islamophobia: Street harassment at the intersections. *Feminist Criminology*, *14*(5), 540–559. https://doi.org/10.1177/1557085118772088

Massey, D. (1984). *Spatial divisions of labour: Social structures and the geography of production*. Methuen.

Massey, D. (2013). Doreen Massey on space. Social Science Bites: A new podcast series with leading social scientists. Sage. Retrieved 17th March 2016 from www.socialsciencebites.com.

Massey, D. (1994). *Space, place and gender*. University of Minnesota Press.

Matrix. (2022). *Making space: Women and the manmade environment*. Verso.

McQuire, S. (1998). *Visions of modernity: Representation, memory, time and space in the age of the camera*. Sage Publications.

Mehta, A., & Bondi, L. (1999). Embodied discourse: On gender and fear of violence. *Gender, Place and Culture*, *6*(1), 67–84. https://doi.org/10.1080/09663699925150

Mellgren, C., Andersson, M., & Anna-Karin, I. (2018). "It happens all the time": Women's experiences and normalization of sexual harassment in public space. *Women & Criminal Justice*, *28*(4), 262–281. https://doi.org/10.1080/08974454.2017.1372328

Menzies, H., & Newson, J. (2007). No time to think: Academics' life in the globally wired university. *Time & Society*, *16*(1), 83–98. https://doi.org/10.1177/0961463X07074103

Middleton, J. (2009). 'Stepping in time': Walking, time and space in the city. *Environment and Planning A*, *41*(8), 1943–1961. https://doi.org/10.1068/a41170

Middleton, J. (2010). Sense and the city: Exploring the embodied geographies of urban walking. *Social and Cultural Geography*, *11*(6), 575–596. https://doi.org/10.1080/14649365.2010.497913

Misztal, B. A. (2003). *Theories of social remembering*. Open University Press.

Mitchell, D. (1995). The end of public space? People's park, definitions of the public and democracy. *Annals of the Association of American Geographers*, *85*(1), 108–133. https://doi.org/10.1111/j.1467-8306.1995.tb01797.x

Morley, D. (2000). *Home territories: Media, mobility and identity*. Routledge.

Mowri, S., & Bailey, A. (2023). Framing safety of women in public transport: A media discourse analysis of sexual harassment cases in Bangladesh. *Media, Culture & Society*, *45*(2), 266–284. https://doi.org/10.1177/01634437221111913

Mulicek, O., Osman, R., & Seidenglanz, D. (2015). Time-space rhythms of the city—The industrial and post-industrial Brno. *Environment and Planning A: Economy and Space*, *48*(1), 115–131. https://doi.org/10.1177/0308518X15594809

Neupane, G., & Chesney-Lind, M. (2014). Violence against women on public transport in Nepal: Sexual harassment and the spatial expression of male privilege. *International Journal of Comparative and Applied Criminal Justice*, *38*(1), 22–38. https://doi.org/10.1080/01924036.2013.794556

Nicholls, E. (2017). 'Dulling it down a bit': Managing visibility, sexualities and risk in the Night Time Economy in Newcastle, UK. *Gender, Place & Culture*, *24*(2), 260–273. https://doi.org/10.1080/0966369X.2017.1298575

Nissen, S. (2008). Urban transformation from public and private space to spaces of hybrid character. *Sociologický Časopis/Czech Sociological Review*, *44*(6), 1129–1149. http://www.jstor.org/stable/41132666

Noor, S., Iamtrakul, P., (2023). Women's access to urban public transport: Toward addressing policy constraints in combating sexual harassment. *Transport Policy*, *137*, 14–22. https://doi.org/10.1016/j.tranpol.2023.04.010

Oakley, A. (1981). Interviewing women: A contradiction in terms? In H. Roberts (Ed.), *Doing feminist research* (pp. 30–61). Routledge.

Oakley, A. (2016). A small sociology of maternal memory. *The Sociological Review, 64*(3), 533–549. https://doi.org/10.1111/1467-954X.12367

Ortlipp, M. (2008). Keeping and using reflective journals in the qualitative research process. *The Qualitative Report, 13*(4), 695–705. https://doi.org/10.46743/2160-3715/2008.1579

Pain, R. (1991). Space, sexual violence and social control: Integrating geographical and feminist analyses of women's fear of crime. *Progress in Human Geography, 15*(4), 415–431. https://doi.org/10.1177/030913259101500403

Pain, R. (1997). Social geographies of women's fear of crime. *Transactions of the Institute of British Geographers, 22*(2), 231–244. http://www.jstor.org/stable/622311

Painter, K. (1992). *Different worlds: The spatial, temporal and social dimensions of female victimisation.* In D. J. Evans, N. R. Fyfe, & D. T. Herbert (Eds.), *Crime, policing and place: Essays in environmental criminology* (pp. 164–195). Routledge.

Peters, K. (2011). Living together in multi-ethnic neighbourhoods: The meaning of space for social integration. Brill Wageningen Academic.

Phadke, S., Khan, S., & Ranade, S. (2011). *Why loiter? Women and risk on Mumbai streets.* Penguin Books.

Pickering, M., & Keightley, E. (2009). Trauma, discourse and communicative limits. *Critical Discourse Studies, 6*(4), 237–249.

Pindek, S., Shen, W., & Andel, S. (2023). Finally, some "me time": A new theoretical perspective on the benefits of commuting. *Organizational Psychology Review, 13*(1), 44–66. https://doi.org/10.1177/20413866221133669

Pratt, A. (2017). The rise of the quasi-public space and its consequences for cities and culture. *Palgrave Communication, 3*(36) https://doi.org/10.1057/s41599-017-0048-6

Prior, N. (2011). Speed, rhythm, and time-space: Museums and cities. *Space and Culture, 14*(2), 197–213. https://doi.org/10.1177/1206331210392701

Poe, E. A. (1840). The man of the crowd. *Burton's Gentleman's Magazine, VII*(6), 267–270.

Pollock, G. (1988). *Vision and difference: Femininity, feminism and the histories of art.* Routledge.

Quinn, B. (2002). Sexual harassment and masculinity: The power and meaning of 'girl watching'. *Gender and Society, 16*(3), 386–402. https://doi.org/10.1177/0891243 202016003007

Rajan, B., Kundu, D., & Sarkar, S. (2022). Rape, Popular Culture, and Nirbhaya: A Study of India's Daughter and Delhi Crime. *Journal of Communication Inquiry, 0*(0). https://doi.org/10.1177/01968599221102527

Rahmanipour, S., Kumar, S., Simon-Kumar, R. (2019) Underreporting sexual violence among 'ethnic'l migrant women: Perspectives from Aotearoa/New Zealand. *Cult Health Sex. 21*(7), 837–852. doi: 10.1080/13691058.2018.1519120

Ramazanoglu, C., & Holland, J. (2002). *Feminist methodology: Challenges and choices.* Sage Publications.

Redmond L. S., & Mokhtarian P. L. (2001). The positive utility of the commute: Modeling ideal commute time and relative desired commute amount. *Transportation, 28*(2), 179–205. https://doi.org/10.1023/A:1010366321778

Reid-Musson, E. (2018) Intersectional rhythmanalysis: Power, rhythm, and everyday life. *Progress in Human Geography, 42*(6), 881–897.

Rizk, J., & Birioukov, A. (2017). Following the flâneur: The methodological possibilities and applications of flânerie in new urban spaces. *The Qualitative Report, 22*(12), 3268–3285. https://doi.org/10.46743/2160-3715/2017.2913

Rospenda, K., Richman, J., & Nawyn, S. (1998). Doing power: The confluence of gender, race and class in contrapower sexual harassment. *Gender and Society, 12*(1), 40–60. https://doi.org/10.1177/089124398012001003

Roth, S., & Newman, E. (1991). The process of coping with sexual trauma. *Journal of Traumatic Stress Behaviour, 4*(2), 279–297. https://doi.org/10.1002/jts.2490040209

Rowe, M. (1974). *"Saturn's Rings" a study of the minutiae of sexism which maintain discrimination and inhibit affirmative action results in corporations and non-profit institutions.* Professional Education of Women, American Association of University Women (pp. 1–9). MIT Sloan.

Salerno-Ferraro, A. C., Erentzen, C., & Schuller, R. A. (2022). Young women's experiences with technology-facilitated sexual violence from male strangers. *Journal of Interpersonal Violence, 37*(19–20), NP17860–NP17885. https://doi.org/10.1177/08862605211030018

Sandberg, L., & Rönnblom, M. (2013). Afraid and restricted vs bold and equal: Women's fear of violence and gender equality discourses in Sweden. *European Journal of Women's Studies, 20*(2), 189–203. https://doi.org/10.1177/1350506812463911

Savard, D. (2018). A routine activity approach: Assessing victimization by gender in transit environments and other public locations. *Advances in Applied Sociology, 8*, 56–75. https://doi.org/10.4236/aasoci.2018.81004

Schneider, B. E. (1991). Put up and shut up: Workplace Sexual Assaults. *Gender & Society, 5*(4), 533–548. https://doi.org/10.1177/089124391005004006

Schwanen, T., van Aalst, I., Brands, J., & Timan, T. (2012). Rhythms of the night; spatiotemporal inequalities in the nighttime economy. *Environment and Planning A: Economy and Space, 44*(9), 2064–2085. https://doi.org/10.1068/a44494

Serlin, D. (2006). Disabling the flâneur. *Journal of Visual Culture, 5*(2), 193–208. https://doi.org/10.1177/1470412906066905

Shaw, R., & Blazek, M. (2023). Politics of rhythm and crisis in the slow death of higher education: implications for academic work and student support. *Critical Studies in Education, 65*(3), 276–293. https://doi.org/10.1080/17508487.2023.2263048

Sheller, M., & Urry, J. (2006). The new mobilities paradigm. *Environment and Planning A: Economy and Space, 38*(2), 207–226. https://doi.org/10.1068/a37268

Shoukry, A., Hassan, R. M., & Komsan, N. A. (2008). *'Clouds in Egypt's Sky'. Sexual harassment: From verbal harassment to rape. A sociological study.* Egyptian Center for Women's Rights.

Skeggs, B. (2004). *Class, self, culture.* Routledge.

Slakoff, D. C. (2022). The mediated portrayal of intimate partner violence in true crime podcasts: Strangulation, isolation, threats of violence, and coercive control. *Violence Against Women, 28*(6–7), 1659–1683. https://doi.org/10.1177/10778012211019055

Simmel, G. (1997). Simmel on Culture. Selected Writings. (Vol 903). Sage Publications.

Simmel, G. (1903). The metropolis and mental life. In G. Bridge & S. Watson (Eds.), *The Blackwell City Reader.* Oxford and Malden: Wiley and Blackwell.

Sinko, L., Munro-Kramer, M., Conley, T., & Saint Arnault, D. (2021). Internalized messages: The role of sexual violence normalization on meaning-making after campus sexual violence. *Journal of Aggression, Maltreatment & Trauma, 30*(5), 565–585. https://doi.org/10.1080/10926771.2020.1796872

Smith, M. J., & Clarke, R. V. (2000). Crime and public transport. *Crime and Justice, 27*, 169–233. http://www.jstor.org/stable/1147664

Smith, O. (2014). *Contemporary adulthood and the night-time economy.* Palgrave Macmillan.

Solnit, R. (2001). *Wanderlust: A history of walking.* Granta Books.

Solymosi, R., Cella, K., & Newton, A. (2017). Did they report it to stop it? A realist evaluation of the effect of an advertising campaign on victims' willingness to report unwanted sexual behaviour. *Security Journal, 31*(2), 570–590. https://doi.org/10.1057/s41284-017-0117-y

Solymosi, R., & Newton, A. (2020). London, UK. In V. Ceccato & A. Loukaitou-Sideris (Eds.), *Transit crime and sexual violence in cities* (pp. 185–195). Routledge.

Sotgiu, I., & Galati, D. (2007). Long-term memory for traumatic events: experiences and emotional reactions during the 2000 flood in Italy. *Journal of Psychology, 141*(1), 91–108. https://doi.org/10.3200/JRLP.141.1.91-108

Spa Future Thinking. (2014). *Safety and security annual report 2013/14.* Spa Future Thinking.

Spiliopoulou, A., & Witcomb, G. L. (2023). An exploratory investigation into women's experience of sexual harassment in the workplace. *Violence Against Women, 29*(9), 1853–1873. https://doi.org/10.1177/10778012221114921

Stanko, E. A. (1993). The case of fearful women: Gender, personal safety and fear of crime. *Women and Criminal Justice, 4*, 117–135. https://doi.org/10.1300/J012V04N01_06

Stanley, L. (2013). *Feminist praxis: Research, theory and epistemology in feminist sociology.* Sage Publications.

Stringer, S. (2007). *Hidden in plain sight: Sexual harassment and assault in the New York City subway system.* Office of the Manhattan Borough President.

Swim, J., & Hyers, L. (1999). Excuse me-what did you just say?!: Women's public and private responses to sexist remarks. *Journal of Experimental Social Psychology, 35*(1), 68–88. https://doi.org/10.1006/jesp.1998.1370

The Standard. (2022). *London transport is ultimate hot bed of sexual harassment.* https://www.standard.co.uk/news/london/london-tube-tfl-sexual-harassment-women-girls-sadiq-khan-zan-moon-b1014464.html#:~:text=Dozens%20of%20women%20have%20come,ultimate%20hotbed%20of%20sexual%20harassment

The Standard. (2023a). *Bystanders to sexual assault on the Tube who do nothing are failing Londoners.* https://www.standard.co.uk/comment/comment/sexual-assault-violence-tube-london-underground-harassment-b1126746.html

The Standard. (2023b). *Police make arrest as 'sex predator' strikes during Elizabeth line chaos.* https://www.standard.co.uk/news/crime/police-arrest-man-women-sex-assault-elizabeth-line-chaos-ladbroke-grove-london-b1125758.html

Thompson, M. J. (2009). What is antiurbanism? A theoretical perspective. In M. J. Thompson (Ed.), *Fleeing the city* (pp. 9–33). Palgrave Macmillan. https://doi.org/10.1057/9780230101050_2

Thrift, N. (1996). *Spatial formations.* Sage Publications.

Tilley, S., & Houston, D. (2016). The gender turnaround: Young women now travelling more than young men. *Journal of Transport Geography, 54*, 349–358. https://doi.org/10.1016/j.jtrangeo.2016.06.022

Transport for London. (2016). *Safety and security annual report 2016.* Future Thinking.

Transport for London. (2024). *What we do.* https://tfl.gov.uk/corporate/about-tfl/what-we-do

Troiani, I., & Dutson, C. (2021). The neoliberal university as a space to learn/think/work in higher education. *Architecture and Culture, 9*(1), 5–23. https://doi.org/10.1080/20507828.2021.1898836

Tromp, S., Koss, M. P., Figueredo, A. J., & Tharan, M. (1995). Are rape memories different? A comparison of rape, other unpleasant and pleasant memories among employed women. *Journal of Traumatic Stress, 8*(4), 607–627. https://doi.org/10.1007/BF02102891

Trust for London. (2024). *London's geography and population.* https://trustforlondon.org.uk/data/geography-population/#:~:text=Ethnic%20group%20populations%2C%202021%20Census.&text=Around%208.9%20million%20people%20live,of%20England%27s%20growth%20of%206.3%25

Tuan, Y. F. (1975). Images and mental maps. *Annals of the Association of American Geographers, 65*(2), 205–213. https:doi.org/10.12691/ajcea-5-3-2

Tuerkheimer, D. (1997). *Street harassment as sexual subordination: The phenomenology of gender-specific harm, 12 Wis. Women's L.J 167* (Paper 177). College of Law Faculty Publications.

UK Parliament. (2018). *Sexual harassment of women and girls in public places inquiry.* https://committees.parliament.uk/work/6031/sexual-harassment-of-women-and-girls-in-public-places-inquiry/publications/

UN Women. (2021). *Public spaces need to be safe and inclusive for all.* Now. https://www.unwomenuk.org/safe-spaces-now/

Urry, J. (2000). Mobile sociology. *The British Journal of Sociology, 51*(1), 185–203. https://doi.org/10.1111/j.1468-4446.2000.00185.x

Urry, J. (2004). The 'system' of automobility. *Theory, Culture & Society, 12*(4–5), 25–39. https://doi.org/10.1177/0263276404046059

Urry, J. (2007). *Mobilities.* Polity Press.

Valan, M. L. (2020). Victimology of sexual harassment on public transportation: Evidence from India. *Journal of Victimology and Victim Justice, 3*(1), 24–37. https://doi.org/10.1177/2516606920927303

Valentine, G. (1990). Women's fear and the design of public space. *Built Environment, 16*(4), 288–303

Vera-Gray, F. (2016). Men's intrusions: Re-thinking street harassment. *Women's Studies International Forum, 58*, 9–17. https://doi.org/10.1016/j.wsif.2016.04.001

Vera-Gray, F. (2018). *The right amount of panic: How women trade freedom for safety.* Policy Press

Vera-Gray, F., & Kelly, L. (2020). Contested gendered space: public sexual harassment and women's safety work. *International Journal of Comparative and Applied Criminal Justice, 44*(4), 265–275. https://doi.org/10.1080/01924036.2020.1732435

Virilio, P. (1986). *Speed and politics: An essay on dromology.* Semiotext.

Volkan, V. (2002). September 11 and societal regression. *Group Analysis, 35*(4), 456–483. https://doi.org/10.1177/05333160260620733

Vostal, F. (2015). Academic life in the fast lane: The experience of time and speed in British academia. *Time & Society, 24*(1), 71–95. https://doi.org/10.1177/0961463X13517537

Warr, M. (1984). Fear of victimization: Why are women and the elderly more afraid? *Social Science Quarterly, 65*(3), 681–702

Watts, L. (2006). *Travel times (or journeys with Ada).* Department of Sociology, Lancaster University. http://eprints.lancs.ac.uk/4348/.

Welsh, S., Carr, J., MacQuarrie, B., & Huntley, A. (2006). 'I'm not thinking of it as sexual harassment' Understanding harassment across race and citizenship. *Gender and Society, 20*(1), 87–107. https://doi.org/10.1177/0891243205282785

Wessendorf, S. (2014). 'Being open, but sometimes closed'. Conviviality in a super-diverse London neighbourhood. *European Journal of Cultural Studies, 17*(4), 392–405. https://doi.org/10.1177/1367549413510415

WHO. (2021). *Violence against women.* https://www.who.int/news-room/fact-sheets/detail/violence-against-women

Wilson, A. E., Gunn, G. R., & Ross, M. (2009). The role of subjective time in identity regulation. *Applied Cognitive Psychology, 23*(8), 1164–1178. https://doi.org/10.1002/acp.1617

Wilson, E. (1991). *The Sphinx in the city: Urban life, the control of disorder and women.* University of California Press.

Wilson, E. (2001). *The contradictions of culture: Cities, culture, women.* Sage Publications.

Wolf, D. (1996). *Feminist dilemmas in fieldwork.* Westview Press.

Wolff, J. (1985). The invisible flâneuse: Women and the literature of modernity. *Theory, Culture and Society, 2*(3), 37–46. https://doi.org/10.1177/0263276485002003005

Woolf, V. (2006). *The London scene.* Random House.

Wosk, J. (2001). *Women and the machine: Representations from the spinning wheel to the electronic age.* John Hopkins University Press.

Young, I. M. (Ed.) (1980) Throwing like a girl: A phenomenology of feminine body comportment motility and spatiality. Human Studies, *3*, 137–156.

Zukin, S. (2009). *Naked city: The death and life of authentic urban places.* Oxford University Press.

www.ingramcontent.com/pod-product-compliance
Lightning Source LLC
Chambersburg PA
CBHW070347270326
41926CB00017B/4019